THE FOURTH GOSPEL REARRANGED

THE FOURTH GOSPEL REARRANGED

by
THOMAS COTTAM

LONDON : THE EPWORTH PRESS

PUBLISHED BY

THE EPWORTH PRESS
(FRANK H. CUMBERS)

25–35 CITY ROAD, LONDON, E.C.1

*

New York · *Toronto*
Melbourne · *Cape Town*

*

Made in Great Britain
First published 1952

SET IN MONOTYPE OLD STYLE AND PRINTED IN
GREAT BRITAIN BY THE CAMELOT PRESS LTD.
LONDON AND SOUTHAMPTON

TO MY WIFE

WITHOUT WHOM THIS STUDY COULD NOT HAVE
BEEN UNDERTAKEN

PREFACE

Dr. James Moffatt's *New Translation of the New Testament* has familiarized the English reader with the idea of a rearrangement of the Fourth Gospel, and other writers have suggested other changes. The present study is an attempt to rearrange some at least of the sections which as found in the traditional text appear to be not in their original order, into an order which it is hoped may in some degree approximate to that designed by the author.

The whole of the Gospel is surveyed, and many suggested rearrangements by modern writers are reviewed—some being adopted, some modified, and others declined; while some now offered are not known to have been previously advocated by others. All such transpositions are necessarily tentative, but those here put forward appear to form a coherent scheme.

Suggestions are also made as to the way in which the traditional order came about; and the new order is compared with the Synoptic Gospels.

The Gospel is taken as it has come down to us, and, apart from any preconceived theory, is interrogated as to its earliest literary history. The result is very different from that expected when this study was first taken in hand.

T. Cottam

Ely, Cambs.
11th February 1952

CONTENTS

This rearrangement brings the guards' report of their non-arrest of Jesus on the same day as the arrest was ordered.

Two ceremonies at Tabernacles: water-carrying and lamp-lighting—The 'last day' of the feast.

The discourse of ch. 9 here continued—Does not suitably follow 7⁵² or 7¹⁵⁻²⁴.

Suitably concludes ch. 9 and 8¹²⁻²⁰.

Continues the speech of vv. 22–9.

Completes the foregoing, and continues the general narrative.

ABBREVIATIONS

AC	*Amicitiae Corolla*, ed. C. H. Dodd
ANT	C. A. Alington, *The New Testament*
BJ	J. H. Bernard, *St John* (*I.C.C.*)
BJP	G. W. Broomfield, *John, Peter, and the Fourth Gospel*
CBE	*Cambridge Biblical Essays*, ed. H. B. Swete
CHE	D. W. Forrest, *The Christ of History and Experience*
CLJ	C. J. Cadoux, *The Life of Jesus*
CJW	J. E. Carpenter, *The Johannine Writings*
DAC	*Dictionary of the Apostolic Church*, ed. J. Hastings
DCG	*Dictionary of Christ and the Gospels*, ed. J. Hastings
DJL	W. F. Lofthouse, *The Disciple whom Jesus loved*
EB	*Encyclopaedia Biblica*
EBr	*Encyclopaedia Britannica*, edn xiv
EGT	*Expositor's Greek Testament*
ERE	*Encyclopaedia of Religion and Ethics*, ed. J. Hastings
ET	*Expository Times*
Exp	*Expositor*
FGG	B. H. Streeter, *The Four Gospels*
FGH	A. C. Headlam, *The Fourth Gospel as History*
FGRC	W. F. Howard, *The Fourth Gospel in Recent Criticism, etc.*
GBD	A. E. Garvie, *The Beloved Disciple*
GHD	V. H. Stanton, *The Gospels as Historical Documents*
GHT	F. C. Burkitt, *The Gospel History and its Transmission*

B

G-S	J. Gardner-Smith, *St John and the Synoptics*
HDB	*Dictionary of the Bible*, ed. J. Hastings
HE	Eusebius, *Ecclesiastical History* (*Historias Ecclesiastices*)
HFG	H. S. Holland, *The Fourth Gospel*
HJ	*Hibbert Journal*
ILNT	J. Moffatt, *Introduction to Literature of N.T.*
INT	A. H. McNeile, *Introduction N.T.*
JGL	C. E. Raven, *Jesus and the Gospel of Love*
JTS	*Journal of Theological Studies*
LQHR	*London Quarterly and Holborn Review*
MJ	G. H. C. Macgregor, *The Gospel of John* (*Moffatt Comm.*)
M & M Voc.	Moulton and Milligan, *Vocabulary of the Greek Testament*
PCB	*Commentary on the Bible*, ed. A. S. Peake
SFG	R. H. Strachan, *The Fourth Gospel*, 3rd (Revised) edn
SMJ	V. Burch, *The Structure and Message of St John's Gospel*
TRJ	W. Temple, *Readings in St John's Gospel*
WJ	F. B. Westcott, *The Gospel accdg to St John* (*Speaker's Comm.*)
XJ	W. F. Howard, *Christianity accdg to St John*

The references to authors in the following pages are not exhaustive, but are representative.

INTRODUCTION

That the Fourth Gospel is very different from the other three is clear to any careful reader; and most modern writers about it have tended to emphasize the differences rather than the similarities: so much so that many have felt unable to rely on it as a historical record, but treat it as some kind of allegory or as an interpretation of the Good News of Christ.

In recent times it has been pointed out that, in addition to obvious comments by the author, many paragraphs read as if they were meditations on the events rather than a record of the Lord's words or deeds. This seems to have been the view taken by the Revisers of 1881 in making 3^{16-21} into a separate paragraph, thus suggesting that it might be a comment of the evangelist and not a record of the words of Jesus.[1]

Further study seemed to show that certain sections of the text were somehow not in their right sequence; and it was noticed that several of these were of about the same length: so the suggestion was made that the original Gospel or a copy of it had in some way become dislocated, perhaps by the roll or codex falling to pieces. An alternative possibility, favoured by some writers, is that there has been an intentional rearrangement of the order of events.

Then, in addition to the author's comments there appear to be certain interpolations by another hand: few in the opinion of some; more numerous in the opinion of others. Some passages also, when read in their traditional position, have raised various questions in respect of authorship and historical value. Restoring these passages to their

[1] See *WJ*, loc. cit.

original places may modify some of the answers that have been given.

In any case, when it has once been said, it seems evident that this Gospel cannot be rightly interpreted till its parts have been properly rearranged.

The theory of displacement usually suggested is that the book containing this Gospel by some means fell to pieces and that someone simply did his best at putting it together again in as good order as he could.

Until recently no very early copy of this or any Gospel was known to exist, and it was supposed that the early Christians, since the apostles were Jews, would follow the Jewish practice of inscribing their Scriptures on a skin or parchment roll. But it is difficult to imagine how or why such a roll should fall to pieces in small sections of fairly equal length. In recent years, however, there have been found in Egypt portions, sometimes mere fragments, of the New Testament written on papyrus, which also was often used in the form of rolls. But these discoveries are usually parts of codices, i.e. books made up of folded sheets like our modern books, e.g. the *Chester-Beatty* papyri.

The dislocations must have occurred early, probably in the original manuscript, as no other order of contents is known; whereas if only one fair duplicate copy had been made, it would, of course, have been copied again and again, and its descendants would in all likelihood be as numerous as those of the dislocated copy, which could then have been compared with the perfect copy and put into correct order. Thus it would appear that there is no plausible alternative to this part of the theory; and if dislocation has occurred it must have taken place before any duplicate had been made.

The general rearrangement here made is not intended to exclude minor rearrangements of the text within the sections. Indeed, it might well be expected that alterations as well as variant readings would result from the displacements, as scribes came across unlooked-for transitions from one subject to another. Several instances are mentioned in the notes, as at $3^{13, 31}$, $4^{1, 2}$, 5^1—and there are others. This study, however, does not seek to deal with the many other places where such alterations have been suggested, except in 1^{1-18} (*q.v.*).

REARRANGEMENTS

As long ago as the second century of our era Tatian in his *Diatessaron* altered the order of a number of passages of this Gospel in order to fit them into his Harmony of the Four; and the Sinaitic Syriac version (fourth century) rearranges several verses in ch. 18; while during the last seventy years or so an increasing number of Continental, British and American scholars have made various rearrangements.

In 1906 F. J. Paul[1] suggested that 7[15-24] should be placed after ch. 5, and that chh. 15 and 16 should come before the end of ch. 14. Similar suggestions occur in R. H. Strachan's article on this Gospel,[2] but in his later book[3] he accepts only the former transposition. A. S. Peake[4] appears to endorse a suggestion by J. Wellhausen that chh. 15 and 16 should come perhaps after 13[32]; ch. 14 connecting immediately with ch. 17. F. Warburton Lewis,[5] starting from the work of F. Spitta (1893 and later), suggests, among other things, in addition to the two rearrangements already mentioned, that ch. 6 should follow immediately on ch. 4, and that 10[1-18] should be placed between 10[29] and 10[30]. V. Taylor[6] and A. E. Garvie[7] accept these four changes and would put 12[44-50] before 12[36b-43]. Moffatt[8] has the above transpositions except that relating to chh. 4 and 6, and also places 18[19-24] after 18[14]. J. H. Bernard[9] accepts all these arrangements, except the last, and puts ch. 4 immediately after 3[22-30]. G. H. C. Macgregor[10] transposes as above, and in addition places 3[31-6] after 3[13]; makes 8[21ff.] follow 7[36]; puts

[1] *HJ*, VII.662ff.   [2] *DCG*.   [3] *SFG*.
[4] *Introduction to the New Testament*, 227
[5] *Disarrangements in the Fourth Gospel*; and *Interpreter*, VIII.109–10.
[6] *The Gospels*.   [7] *GBD*.   [8] *New Translation N.T.*   [9] *BJ*.   [10] *MJ*.

3^{14-21} into ch. 12; and in ch. 18 places v. 24 after v. 13, and transposes vv. 16–18 and 19–23. The two last-named writers also suggest that the Cleansing of the Temple (and, Bernard, the Nicodemus interview) probably belongs to the close of the public ministry of Jesus. F. W. Lewis, in a later work,[11] also puts $2^{23}–3^{11}$ into ch. 12. These rearrangements, with some modifications, are included in the present scheme.

Many writers, including some of those mentioned, have made other suggestions: 3^{22-30} is usually taken out of its present context and placed in some new position; ch. 5 is often put after ch. 6; while $7^{53}–8^{11}$, separated by the Revisers from the body of the Gospel, owing to its not being found in any of the best Greek manuscripts, is usually dropped out altogether. W. F. Howard[12] gives a summary of textual displacements suggested by several writers.

Only so much of the Gospel text is given in the following pages as serves to show how the parts fit together in the new order.

[11] *Jesus, Saviour of Man.*   [12] *FGRC*, App. D.

THE SECTIONS AS REARRANGED

SECTION 1

1¹–2¹³ᵃ.—It has been recognized in recent years that part of the Prologue (1¹⁻¹⁸) is poetical in structure after the Hebrew model, although there is much difference of opinion as to the extent of this poetry. In the present arrangement only vv. 6–8 and 15, which refer to the Baptist, are not included in it. Macgregor[1] suggests that the original order was vv. 1–5, 9–14, 16–18. C. Cryer[2] gives the same list except that he omits 12ᵈ and 13ᶜ. The poem appears to consist of three parts or stanzas of some eleven lines each, together with a concluding stanza of some half-dozen lines: (I) vv. 1–5, (II) vv. 9–12, (III) vv. 13, 14, 16, (IV) vv. 17, 18.

Each stanza begins with the statement of a great fact concerning 'the Word', and in successive stanzas these facts progress from eternity to time. The first announces the eternal existence of the Word; the second, that he 'was coming into the world'; the third, the manner of his coming; and the fourth identifies him with the historical Jesus Christ. The latter part of each stanza, except the last, likewise expresses the result on human life of these facts, and progress is made from the general to the particular: (i) 'the life was the light of men'; (ii) 'his own people received him not. But as many as received him . . .'; (iii) 'we beheld his glory . . . of his fullness did we all receive.' The fourth stanza is a kind of summary, and its conclusion is the rest of the Gospel. The prose narrative begins after the ending of the poem with vv. 6–8, 15, 19ff., in this order.[3]

---

[1] *MJ, loc. cit.*   [2] *ET*, XXXII.440–3.   [3] See *FGRC*, 132; also *GBD*, 2.

In the beginning there existed the Word,
And the Word was with God,
And the Word was himself God:
He existed in the beginning with God.

All things were made through him,
And apart from him there was made
Not even one thing that has been made.

In him was life,
And the life was the light of men;
And the light shines in the darkness,
And yet the darkness did not apprehend it.

.   .   .   .   .

The Light, the real Light,
Which enlightens every man,
Was coming into the world.

He was in the world,
And the world was made through him,
And yet the world did not recognize him.

He came to his own home,
And yet his own people did not accept him;
But as many as received him—
To them he gave authority to become children of God—
Even to them that believe in his name.

.   .   .   .   .

Not of blood,
Nor of the desire of the flesh,
Nor of the desire of man,
But of God was he begotten.

And so the Word became flesh
And dwelt among us—
And we beheld his glory:
Glory befitting the Only-begotten One from the Father—
Full of grace and truth.

For out of his fullness did we all receive,
Even grace upon grace.

.   .   .   .   .

For the Law was given through Moses;
Grace and truth came through Jesus Christ.

No man has seen God at any time:
The Only-begotten One, himself God—
He that is in the bosom of the Father—
He has revealed him.

> There appeared a man, sent from God, whose name
> was John. He came for testimony, to testify to the
> Light, that all might believe through him. He him-
> self was not the Light, but he came to testify to the
> Light. John testifies to him and cries aloud, saying,
> 'He that comes after me has taken precedence of me;
> for he was before me'. And this is the testimony
> of John. . . .

In v. 13 all the oldest MSS. known to us, except D, read,
'who [*plural*] . . . were begotten'; and apparently v. 12
contains the antecedent. The *Curetonian* Syriac version
reads, 'who [*plural*] . . . was begotten [*singular*]'. The
Old Latin *b* reads, 'who . . . was born [all singular]',
apparently referring to 'the Word'; and this reading seems
to have been known to Justin (possibly read in seven

places in his works) and Irenaeus (in four places in the
Latin). D omits 'who', and reads, 'they were begotten'.
The Old Latin *a* also omits 'who', and reads, 'they were
born'. Tertullian omits 'who', and reads, 'he was born',
explicitly rejecting the reference to v. 12. Augustine in
his *Confessions* quotes: 'Not of flesh, not of blood, not of
the will of man, neither of the will of the flesh, but of
God was he born.' *The Epistula Apostolorum* (second
century) reads, 'He is the Word made flesh, born in the
sacred Virgin's womb, conceived by the Holy Ghost, not
by carnal lust, but by the will of God' (*FGG*, 70). It is
unlikely that the readings found in most later copies are
correct, since variations tend to drift away from the
archetype rather than toward it.

The reading of Tertullian is adopted here as having
most probability. It is true that the evidence of the extant
Greek MSS. is overwhelmingly against it, but the three
writers first mentioned in support of the singular verb
lived well within a century of the writing of this Gospel
and more than a century before our earliest surviving
MSS. (apart from fragments) were written; while Tertullian
states that copies having his reading actually existed.[4] It
is even said that A. Loisy 'shows that the reading found
in Justin and Irenaeus must be original'.[5] And C. C.
Terry[6] translates 1[12-13]: '. . . to those believing on the
name of him who was born not of blood . . .'; and speaks
of the usual wording as 'a very disturbing mistranslation.
. . . The *di* at the beginning of the verse was singular
number, referring to the pronoun immediately preceding
—the only connexion which the strong language of the
verse makes possible.' W. Temple[7] says: 'Nothing can explain the quite peculiar phrasing of this passage except the

[4] See A. S. Peake, in *PCB*, where Harnack also is quoted.
[5] *HJ*, II.620.
[6] *The Four Gospels; a New Translation.*   [7] *TRJ*, 13.

supposition that it refers to the Virgin Birth of our Lord.'

To refer v. 13 to 'the Word' accords with v. 14, where it is not only said that He 'became flesh', but He is spoken of as 'the Only-begotten One', as again in v. 18. Hoskyns (*The Fourth Gospel*, 164) notes that 'And' links v. 14 closely to v. 13. In v. 12 some are given 'authority to become children of God' because they 'received him' and 'believe in his name'. A further four-fold, largely negative, explanation of their spiritual origin seems quite superfluous. Why, indeed, should anybody suppose that those who have 'become children of God' could have become such through 'blood, or the desire of the flesh, or the desire of man', especially when it has just been stated that it was by a gift from 'the Word' and through faith (cf. Ephesians 2⁸)? It would appear therefore that this verse does not refer to the regeneration of the souls of believers, but to the way in which 'the Word became flesh'—the triple denial deliberately excluding the possibility of any kind of agency other than the Divine. The poetic form of the prologue not being recognized, the words were misunderstood to refer to 'the children of God' mentioned in the previous verse. The *Curetonian* Syriac may illustrate the origin of the error: the scribe having written v. 12, read, 'not of blood', etc., and thinking these words referred to 'them that believe in his name', inserted 'who' as being required to complete the sense, but at the end of the verse copied the *singular* 'was begotten', which he found in his exemplar. With the stanzaic arrangement, however, it is appropriate that the third stanza, like the first and second, should begin with a direct reference to 'the Word'. Macgregor notes that the usual construction is awkward if it refers to v. 12; and Meyer's *Commentary on John* also seems to feel the difficulty, then passes on—the question of rearrangement not then having arisen.

In 1 John 5[18], as here, 'He that was begotten of God'
is mentioned immediately after 'every one that has been
begotten of God'; and the statement has been misunderstood in the same way—a number of codices reading, 'he
. . . keeps himself' for 'he . . . keeps him'. Except in
reported speech the phrase 'was begotten of'—*aorist* with
ek—occurs in the Johannine writings only at 1[13] and
1 John 5[18]. The *perfect* with *ek*, however, is found in
1 John: the *indicative* at 2[29], 3[9], 4[7], and 5[1]; and the *parti-
ciple* at 3[9] and 5[1] (in both instances alongside the *indicative*), and at 5[4] and 5[18]. All the *perfects* refer to believers;
and the *aorists* would appear to be intended to refer to
Christ.[8] John is always careful to use the term 'Son' only
in reference to Jesus, and uses 'children' when writing
of believers. Macgregor[9] notes that 'John always dis-
tinguishes the sense in which Christ and men are "sons"
of God—even using different words'.

The verses 6–8 and 15 are here excluded from the poem.
The former paragraph follows the first stanza, about which
there is a certain completeness; and if no more had been
given we should hardly have suspected that anything was
lacking. Possibly that was all of the poem that the author
had in mind when he began his work, and so, when he
had written vv. 1–5, he went on with the narrative relating
to the Forerunner (vv. 6–8). Verse 5—'shines'—would
seem to support this, the writer having thereby brought
down the preamble to his own times, which may also be
indicated by the *aorist* tense of 'the darkness apprehended
it not'. Strachan[10] says: '[John's] mind is not moving
only in the super-terrestrial world in verses 4 and 5. With
v. 4 his thought begins to circle around the human life
of Jesus. . . . As incarnate, Jesus is the life and the
light of men.' Afterwards the poem expanded itself in

[8] See G. G. Findlay's *Fellowship in the Life Eternal*, 419–21.
[9] *MJ*, 359.   [10] *SFG*, 99.

the author's mind, and the other stanzas were added. K. Lake[11] and others suggest that the prologue may have been written later than the rest of the Gospel.

Verses 7 and 8 (with v. 6, of course) read as if they were meant to follow v. 5. As here rearranged, however, the words, 'the light' (vv. 4 and 5) seem too far away to have been the point of reference. But if our surmise is correct, the original poem included only vv. 1–5 (cf. Luke's preface—Luke 1[1-4]; also 1 John 1[1-4]), so that vv. 6–8 follow naturally after it. Perhaps these words about 'the light' (vv. 4, 5, 7, 8) started the train of thought which produced the rest of the poem: 'The Light, the real Light. . . .'

Signs of dislocation leading to various readings occur in v. 15, where, after 'saying', several good MSS. insert, 'This was he of whom I said'; a few of the best read, 'This was', and insert 'who' before 'has taken precedence'. It would seem that at least some of these words were interpolated, perhaps by a scribal error, from v. 30, and were afterwards altered more than once in the attempt to make them read sensibly; and that the original may have had none of these readings: 'John testifies . . . saying, He that comes after me has taken precedence. . . .' A similar addition is made in v. 27, where אB omit. A. H. McNeile[12] says: 'John's witness to himself [in v. 15] is an awkward parenthesis referring by anticipation to his words in v. 30.' Again, v. 16 begins with *hoti* (for, or, because), so does not suitably follow v. 15; whilst v. 19 begins with 'And', which would appear to connect it with v. 15.

[11] *Introduction to the New Testament*, 61. See also Strachan, *The Historic Jesus*, 131.
[12] *INT*, 262.

SECTION 2

2¹³ᵃ   And the passover of the Jews was near,

5¹ᵇ   and Jesus went up to Jerusalem.

2   Now there is at Jerusalem by the Sheepgate a
         pool . . .

N.B.—The ruled line indicates the break between sections.

5₁₋₄₇.—In many modern rearrangements of John, ch. 5
is placed after ch. 6. Moffatt, however, does not include
this transposition in his *New Translation*, even in the
Revised Edition.

Now the fact that Jesus wrought several of His cures
on the sabbath seems to point to some particular reason.
He had been familiar with the traditional misuse of the
sabbath all His life, and evidently fundamentally disagreed
with it. It cut at the root of true religion, leading men to
suppose that God cared for externals rather than for the
real good of His human children. Hence He made it a
test as to whether men would hold to their mechanical
views or would admit the human, and really divine, interpretation of life.[1] The healing of the man with the
withered hand (Mark 3¹⁻⁶) would seem to be a test case
deliberately put by Jesus to the authorities in Galilee.
After several sabbath incidents, which in the end resulted
in the definite opposition of the Pharisees, it is thought
by some that He may have sought to try out the matter
at Jerusalem, and that ch. 5 may be the record of His
visit.

Now ch. 6 comes at the end of 'the year of public
favour', and is dated at the Passover. Jesus is well known
and is even being sought after by the religious, and perhaps the civil, authorities in Galilee for His destruction.

[1] See Stalker's *Life of Christ*, paras. 126–7; also *CLJ*, 115–16.

It does not seem possible that the religious authorities in Jerusalem would not be fully aware of all this, since a number of their representatives had been in conflict with Him in Galilee for some time past. Some rearrangements date ch. 5 at the Passover, said to be 'near' at 6⁴, or at the following Pentecost, only some four months before the feast of Tabernacles. When, however, Jesus appears at the latter feast everybody is speculating about Him (7¹¹⁻¹³), and 'some of the Jerusalemites said, Is not this he whom they are wanting to kill?' (7²⁵). In fact, several attempts are made to arrest Him (7³⁰, ³², ⁴⁴).

But in ch. 5 everything is different. In spite of 'a crowd being at the place', Jesus is unrecognized.² No mention is made of disciples: there cannot have been anything like twelve about Him, or He could not so easily have 'moved away' unnoticed. 'The Jews' know nothing of Jesus, but ask 'Who is it?' and for a time receive no answer. The man himself does not know, but, some time later (*meta tauta*), not immediately, after Jesus had found him and had spoken to him, he innocently tells them: 'It is Jesus.' It is certain that after ch. 6 the authorities would not need to be told. Again, the words, 'He that made me well' (v. 11), do not suggest to their minds anything extraordinary such as a 'work of power' or a 'sign'. The healer might have been any physician. Contrast this with 'What are we doing? For this man is doing many signs' (11⁴⁷). The incident does not appear to have been noticed even by the other sufferers, or by 'the crowd' who were 'at the place'. The first questioning arose not on account of the healing, but because of the man's carrying his pallet (vv. 11–13). In v. 20 Jesus says, 'that you may wonder' —they had not 'wondered' at the healing of the sick man, for they had not noticed it. So far they had only had the man's word to go on as to his having been made well.

² *GBD*, 44, where Garvie notes several of these points.

The *imperfect* tenses of v. 16 may indicate the beginning of the action: 'For this reason the Jews began to persecute Jesus because he began to do these things on the sabbath.' Nothing of the kind had been done before on either side. M. Dods[3] paraphrases: 'They began from this point to meditate hostile action.'

When we look at the beginning of the ministry in Capernaum, but never afterwards, we find the same general conditions as at the beginning of ch. 5—everything is obviously new and unexpected. In Mark 1[25-6], in the absence of any 'authorities' from Jerusalem (since no one knew that Jesus was going to begin preaching in Galilee), no opposition is aroused by His healing of the demoniac on the sabbath; but 'they were all amazed . . . they said, What is this? A new teaching!' But by the time of the healing of the man with the withered hand (Mark 3[2]) the Pharisees are keenly alert on the point: 'They watched him, whether he would heal on the sabbath, that they might accuse him.' And shortly afterwards 'the scribes who had come from Jerusalem' (Mark 3[22]) were ready to find fault with everything He did, and said, 'He has Beelzebul', and, 'By the prince of the demons he casts out the demons'. If, later, He had healed on the sabbath in Jerusalem, the Jews would at once have recognized both the healing and the Healer, as indeed they do in the case of the man born blind (9[1]), when the blind man, his parents, the Pharisees, and 'the Jews', all know who Jesus is and what is His attitude to life.

To sum up: In ch. 5 Jesus (a) is not personally known either to the populace or to the authorities, (b) is not known as a worker of miracles, and (c) probably has not yet any definite body of disciples (apostles). These considerations appear to rule out the later period of the ministry, when numbers both of admirers and of opponents

[3] *EGT.*

followed Him about, and when everybody was talking about Him (7^{11-13}, etc.).

Again, it would seem that 4^{45} must refer to a time before Jesus had wrought any work of healing in Galilee. 4^{54} says: 'This again, a second sign, did Jesus after coming from Judæa to Galilee'—that is, except for that of 2^{1-11}, no sign had been wrought there before this of 4^{46-53}.[4] Otherwise the Galileans would have been able to match 'all the things which he did in Jerusalem' with as great works already done in their own province. As traditionally arranged, apart from the general statement of 2^{23}, which our scheme puts much later (see §18), John has no record of any healing previous to 4^{45} either at Jerusalem or elsewhere. Bernard[5] notes that no healings have yet occurred to account for 2^{23}. Now, although he assumes a general knowledge of the Gospel story on the part of his readers, yet John could hardly have made such a statement as he does in 4^{45} without giving some instance of what he meant. Ch. 5 would supply the instance if placed somewhere before that point. But 4^{1-54} appears to follow naturally on 3^{22-30} without any considerable interval, so that, if ch. 5 precedes ch. 4, it should also probably precede 3^{22}. 'He came into Galilee' (4^{45}) seems to refer to the same occasion as Mark 1^{14}: 'After John had been arrested Jesus came into Galilee' to begin His ministry there.[6] Hence the events of ch. 5 must have occurred before this—during the ministry of John; for 'John was baptizing at Ænon' (3^{23}).

If then our rearrangement is correct, ch. 5 records the first of our Lord's acts of healing. The first could not have been that of the officer's son, since the officer obviously came to Jesus because he had heard of 'the things he did in Jerusalem'. So unless we accept ch. 5 as recording the first healing or else assume that the record is not

[4] cf. *ET*, LVII.218.   [5] *BJ*, 98.   [6] *CLJ*, 89.

in any Gospel—a desperate assumption, since the first of such acts would become widely known (cf. 4⁴⁵ and Mark 1³²⁻³)—then we must look elsewhere: the only answer apparently being in Mark 1²³ff. But here again, if Jesus were not known to heal, why should the afflicted man think He was going to interfere in his case? As no one knew anything of His healing power no one could expect Him to heal until something had occurred to suggest it to them. So that the initiative must have come from Jesus Himself. With the exceptions of the bent woman (Luke 13¹¹⁻¹³) and Malchus' ear (Luke 22⁵⁰⁻¹) all other instances of bodily healing on the part of Jesus are introduced to His notice by others. Even these two exceptions are cases where the matter is thrust on His notice by the immediate circumstances.

But in ch. 5 Jesus takes the initiative and selects (5⁶: 'when he had ascertained') from a considerable number this particular man for healing. It is the only occurrence of its kind recorded in any Gospel where Jesus clearly makes the first move, without any outside suggestion; and it is thus marked out as the first instance. F. R. M. Hitchcock[7] remarks on 'the voluntary nature of the cure'. On His seeking to change the harsh sabbatarianism of the Pharisees Jesus sought to appease their expected opposition and gain their sympathy by choosing a man who had been ill some thirty-eight years (cf. Luke 13¹⁶). He seems to have retained His hope of modifying the traditional view well into His ministry. Even when the definite break with the Pharisees took place (Mark 3¹⁻⁶)[8] He was still hoping for some sign of mercy from them, but found none; for when 'they kept silence', He 'looked round about on them with anger, being grieved at the hardening of their heart'. In the instance given in Luke 14²⁻⁶ He did shame them so that at any rate they made no outward

[7] DCG, I.412b.   [8] GHT, 68–9.

protest when He healed the dropsical man on the sabbath, challenging their sympathy by comparing him to 'an ox fallen into a well'. J. A. Findlay[9] says: 'The note of this early and long-sustained attempt to come to an understanding with the religious leaders of Jerusalem . . . may be found in John 5[19]. . . . So far from its being true that . . . in the first five chapters of the Fourth Gospel the claim Jesus makes for Himself is more advanced than that made in the Synoptic Gospels, the real truth is the other way round. In the Fourth Gospel Jesus argues for and expounds the claim which He *takes for granted* in the Synoptics.'

That the events of ch. 5 took place in the very early ministry is supported by the statements of vv. 32–5, where He says: 'It is another who *testifies* to me, and I know that the testimony is valid which he *testifies* to me.' This, of course, refers to God the Father, who is expressly mentioned in v. 37. Note that the tenses of v. 32 are *present*. At this point He perceives that His hearers think He is speaking of the Baptist, who did witness to Him, so He says: 'You *have sent* to John and he *has testified* to the truth.' Now if John were not alive and still witnessing there would have been no reason for the Jews to think the words referred to Him. Note that in v. 33 the tenses are *perfect* and cannot be interpreted as *aorist*: the witness continues. The second of these words is repeated in v. 37 of the Father, whose witness certainly cannot be confined to the past.

Now Mark 6[21-9] makes the death of John to precede the Feeding of the Five Thousand; so that both the *present* and the *perfect* tenses of vv. 32–3 would be incorrect if ch. 5 were to follow ch. 6. John 10[41]: 'John *did* no sign, but what John *said* about this man *was* true'—the *past* tenses are correct; for the Baptist's testimony had ceased.

9 *What did Jesus teach?*, 168–9.

The *past* tenses of 5³⁵, 'He *was* the lamp that burns and shines, and you *were willing* for an hour to rejoice in his light', do not rule out this interpretation—the reason for them being that the Baptist was only 'the lamp' and his 'hour' is over; for 'the real Light is now shining'.

That ch. 5 belongs to the early ministry is further supported by vv. 19ff. This is Jesus' *Apologia* offered on the occasion of the first challenge to His actions. B. F. Westcott[10] says: 'The discourse in ch. v. . . . is the recorded beginning of Christ's prophetic teaching. He unfolds the nature of His work and His Person in answer to the first accusations of the Jews. . . . It is . . . the outline of a systematic defence. . . . It deals . . . with just those topics which belong to the beginnings of the great controversy at Jerusalem.' 'He made his defence (*apekrinato*)'[11] is found in John only at 5¹⁷, ¹⁹, and seems to indicate a formal occasion. No doubt He defended His doings later on (7²⁸, 8²⁸, etc.), but not with anything like the same fullness. Here He declares that what He had done was no choice of His own: He simply and necessarily did what God willed to be done, because (*a*) He was so closely associated with God as 'the Son' to 'the Father'; and (*b*) the Father was continually showing Him His will. His obedience and therefore His actions arose of necessity from these facts.[12] He enunciates the principle in v. 19, and expounds it in vv. 20–9 as including such high matters as resurrection and judgement. Then in v. 30 He applies the principle to Himself as an individual in the case under discussion: 'I can do nothing of myself: even as I hear I judge; for I seek not my own will, but the will of him that sent me.'

Confirmation that ch. 5 belongs to the early ministry is also found in what it does not contain. In the Synoptics,

[10] *WJ*, Intro.II.6.3.   [11] Abbott: *Johannine Grammar*, 2537.
[12] cf. H. R. Mackintosh, *Person of Jesus Christ*, 326–7.

except the veiled reference to the Bridegroom's being taken away, Jesus mentions neither the fact nor the manner of His departure till after Peter's confession, but from then on His coming death is frequently alluded to. In John likewise there are several occasions when He speaks of His decease, the first being in ch. 6, where a confession of faith by Peter is also recorded. But 5 and 7¹⁵⁻²⁴ are entirely free from any reference of this nature. This agrees with our scheme, but not with the arrangement which puts ch. 5 after ch. 6.

The Temptation shows that in the days succeeding His Baptism Jesus had to face up to His own Person and Mission;[13] and that He was tempted to cast Himself down from the wing of the Temple would seem to indicate that He had Jerusalem in view as the scene of His work and witness. If our chronology is correct the visit to Jerusalem (ch. 5) took place within about a month of the Temptation and consequently within about two months of His Baptism. In this discourse Jesus may be making objective to His own mind all the implications for Himself which were involved in those events. Even in His case all the thoughts about Himself and His work could not be assimilated at once, but one conclusion would lead to another; and there is nothing like challenge for opening up the connotation of any theory. Most of the arguments used to support the idea of an appeal or a challenge to the authorities in Jerusalem at the beginning of the ministry are applicable to the healing of ch. 5 as much as to the Cleansing of the Temple. The conclusion appears to be that ch. 5 belongs to the very earliest stages of the ministry of Jesus. Hence this section is here placed after 2¹³ᵃ.

In our arrangement 5¹ᵃ is superfluous and is omitted. It may have been inserted only after the sections had

[13] *GHT*, 77.

been arranged by the editor and when the fair copy was being written out. In the traditional text it suitably supplements the narrative. In 4⁴⁶⁻⁵⁴ Jesus is in Galilee, but in 5¹ᵇ we read: 'and Jesus went up to Jerusalem.' The editor perhaps recognized that John never uses '*kai (and)*' . . . to begin a fresh incident, so that here was required some introductory statement, and simply said: 'After these things there was a feast of the Jews.' On the other sixteen occasions of its use in John the word 'feast' always has the article, which is here omitted. That the feast is not named suggests that the editor did not know which it was. But as Garvie says:[14] 'The witness was too familiar himself with Jewish affairs not to be able to name this feast.' The second half of 5¹ is retained as original and follows the first half of 2¹³.[15]

Alternatively, it is possible that the original draft read as follows:

2¹³	And near was the Passover, the
5¹	feast of the Jews, and went up Jesus to Jerusalem.

N.B.—The phrase, 'the Passover, the feast of the Jews', occurs again at 6⁴.

If the above division of the words is correct, 5¹ could be completed as in the traditional text merely by prefixing '*Meta tauta ēn* (After these things there was [*a* feast of the Jews])'—the indefinite article was not used in Greek, but is required in English.

In 2¹³ the word 'the' at the end of the line may have been absent, in which case the words, 'of the Jews' would be supplied by the editor; but if it was present it would be represented by a single letter formed like our capital H. Occurring as it does, according to our rearrangement, at the end of a page which was followed by a page not in continuation of the narrative, it would have no meaning;

[14] *GBD*, 45.   [15] *ET*, XXXVIII.91–2.

and if perhaps it was not carefully written (cross-strokes are apt to be misplaced) the editor may have read it as TI, and have interpreted it as constituting the initials of TŌN IOUDAIŌN (of the Jews), which thus became part of the traditional text. Such abbreviations are common, even in fair copies of ancient writings, and are much more likely in a first draft not copied out 'fair'. The same phrase, 'the Passover of the Jews', is found again at 11[55].

SECTION 3

5[46] . . . if you believed Moses you would believe me;
[47] for it was of me that he wrote. But if you believe not his writings, how shall you believe my sayings?

7[15] The Jews therefore began to wonder, saying, 'How does this man know the writings, since he has not been taught [i.e. in the Rabbinical schools]?

N.B.—*Grammata* (Writings) occurs in John only at 5[47] and 7[15].[1]

7[15-24].—While there is nothing in 7[1-14] to account for 7[15], there is exactly what is needed in 5[46-7]. This arrangement is generally admitted.[2] That the Jews here wonder that Jesus is well acquainted with the Old Testament Scriptures suggests that the incident happened in His early ministry, because, later, they were made fully aware of it by His apt quotations directed to themselves. Verse 20 indicates that the people in general knew of no serious hostility to Jesus on the part of the authorities. (J. M. Thompson[3] points out that this verse disagrees with v. 25.) Consequently this section must belong to the early days,

[1] cf. A. M. Hunter, *DCG*, II.26b.   [2] *BJ*, xix–xx.
[3] *Exp*, VIII.ix.423.

since their opposition became well known later on, as at 7^{25}, etc.

When 5 and 7^{15-24} are put between chh. 6 and 7 it is sometimes argued that 7^1, 'the Jews were seeking to kill him', is the sequel to 7^{19}: 'Why do you seek to kill me?' But this takes no account of the answer of the crowd (7^{20}), 'You are mad: who wants to kill you?' on the one hand; and on the other hand, of the question of another crowd (7^{25}), 'Is not this the man they want to kill?' Obviously the circumstances are quite different.

'I did one work' (v. 21) supports the early date of both 5 and 7^{15-24}. Of course, it could be read as 'one in this city', or, 'one just now'; but these phrases do not seem to express the real meaning of the words.

We note the following parallels:

5^{8-9}	[The healing of the infirm man.]
7^{23}	I made an entire man well.

5^{18}	The Jews wanted . . . to kill him.
7^{19}	Why do you want to kill me?

5^{19}	The Son can do nothing of himself, but only what he sees the Father doing.
5^{30}	I can do nothing of my own accord.
7^{16}	My teaching is not mine, but his that sent me.

5^{30}	As I hear I judge, and my judgement is righteous.
7^{24}	Judge righteous judgement.

5^{36}	The works . . . testify.
5^{37}	The Father . . . has testified.
5^{39}	The scriptures . . . testify to me.
7^{17}	He shall know . . . whether it is from God.

5⁴¹ Glory from man I do not accept.
5⁴³ I have come in the name of my Father.
5⁴⁴ The glory which is from God you do not seek.
7¹⁸ He that seeks the glory of him that sent him is true.

5⁴⁵ One accuses you—Moses.
5⁴⁶ Of me he spoke.
7¹⁹ Moses gave you the Law.

5⁴⁷ If you do not believe his writings.
7¹⁵ How does this man know the writings?

SECTION 4

3²²⁻³⁰.—As found in the traditional order this section seems to be out of place. Many have recognized that it comes well before ch. 4, a sequence obtained simply by removing 3³¹⁻⁶. But what it follows is not so easy to determine. In some rearrangements it comes after 2¹²,[1] the passage then reading: 'After this [first visit to Cana] he went down to Capernaum, he and his mother and brothers, and his disciples; and there they remained not many days. After these things Jesus and his disciples came into the country district of Judaea. . . .' But we expect something to have occurred to account for 'After these things', but nothing is mentioned. Again, 3²³ leans to the probability that some time more than the 'not many days' of 2¹² had elapsed since 1²⁸ᶠᶠ·; for John has left his former preaching-place (cf. 10⁴⁰), and is now located west of the Jordan (cf. 'he that was with you on the other side of Jordan'—3²⁶), and 'they were coming to him and being baptized'. Obviously this must precede Mark 1¹⁴.

[1] Bernard rejects this arrangement, *BJ*, xxiv.

Moreover, if Jesus came here from Galilee there would have been no reason for saying, 'the country district of Judaea', as 'Judaea' would have sufficed. It would seem rather that 'the country district' was mentioned in contrast to Jerusalem, as at 11⁵⁴, where Jesus leaves Bethany —near Jerusalem—for 'the country', and 11⁵⁵, where 'many went up to Jerusalem out of the country'; also cf. Luke 21²¹: 'Let not those who are in the country enter into [Jerusalem].' The most natural interpretation of the words would appear to be that Jesus left the city and went into the country parts of Judaea. Both Bernard and Macgregor interpret in this way, though in a different context. To place 3²²⁻³⁰ after ch. 5 and 7¹⁵⁻²⁴ fulfils the conditions; but only if the two latter sections are put before the beginning of the ministry in Galilee.

SECTION 5

3²⁶   'Rabbi, he that was with you on the other side of Jordan . . . see, he is baptizing, and everybody
²⁷   is coming to him.' John answered and said . . .
³⁰   '. . . He must increase, but I must decrease'.

4¹   When, then, the Lord knew that the Pharisees had heard, 'Jesus is making and baptizing more disciples than John' . . .

³   he forsook Judaea and departed again for Galilee.

N.B.—The phrase 'the Lord' is probably not original either here or at 6²³ or 11².

4¹⁻⁵⁴.—As suggested in the notes on §4, this section seems to follow immediately on 3³⁰ (3³¹⁻⁶ goes to division V). C. J. Cadoux[1] effects this by exchanging 3²²⁻³⁰ and 3³¹⁻⁶

[1] *JTS*, July 1919, p. 317.

(and Bernard also[2] approves), and says: 'The reference to John's baptism and the complaint of John's disciples about Jesus' success are brought into fitting connexion with 4[1f.]' That it belongs to the early ministry is confirmed by the report which reached the Pharisees that 'Jesus is making . . . more disciples than John'—which appears to imply that John is still 'making disciples'. Also, after the start of the preaching in Galilee, everybody knew of the immense crowds which flocked to hear Jesus, and no 'report' was needed. Then there is the statement of v. 8 that 'the disciples had gone off to the town to buy food'. Surely it did not require twelve men to do this: two or three would suffice, say James and Judas Iscariot, the latter known to have held the money-box (12[6], 13[29]), leaving only John with the Master.

The saying of 4[44], 'A prophet has no honour in his own country', is found also in each of the Synoptics in reference to Nazareth. But here in John at first thought it appears to refer to Judaea (it could not refer to Samaria), and seems to mean that Jesus left that province because they had not 'honoured' Him by receiving His prophetic message, especially as we know that Judaea was His own [native] country. But if this had been intended the words would have been much better placed in v. 3: 'he forsook Judaea; for Jesus himself testified. . . .'

The saying would seem to belong to the Rejection at Nazareth narrated by Luke; indeed it is difficult to see how it could apply to anywhere else, since no other place could at that time have been spoken of as 'his own country', while He Himself was everywhere known as 'Jesus of Nazareth'. John may be endorsing Luke's order in placing the incident before the beginning of the ministry in Capernaum. Matthew 4[13] states that 'forsaking Nazareth he came and dwelt at Capernaum'. That Matthew here uses the form 'Nazara', and its only other occurrence in the New Testament is at Luke 4[16], suggests that the document known as 'Q' placed the affair at Nazareth before the Capernaum ministry as does Luke.[3] Matthew omits the incident, as he frequently does omit anything apparently derogatory to Jesus, but appears to have retained part of the context as found in 'Q'.[4] The difficulty is that the 'sign' next narrated would seem to have taken place before and not after the visit to Nazareth, since the challenge is: 'Do here the things we heard were done in Capernaum' (Luke 4[23]). But if John had told of the healing of the officer's son after v. 43, then v. 44 would fit in very awkwardly after v. 54. So it was much the best to put it where it is, following the first mention of Jesus' return to Galilee, since John had no intention of telling the story of Nazareth. It is of course possible that v. 44 was added first in the margin. The places visited would then be, successively, Jerusalem, Judaea, Samaria, Cana, Nazareth, Capernaum.

The statement of 4[45]—'The Galileans welcomed him; for they had seen all the things which he did in Jerusalem at the feast; for they themselves came to the feast'— reads as if the events there were quite recent. But a Judaean ministry is mentioned in 3[22-30], previous to the journey through Samaria. This may have been of only brief duration, and 'the feast' may have been the Passover (2[13], 5[1]). On the other hand, 3[22] says, 'He continued with them'—apparently for some time; for the Baptist's disciples say: 'See, he is baptizing and everybody is coming to him.' And even the Pharisees heard that 'Jesus is making and baptizing more disciples than John'. Some modern writers suggest that for a time Jesus

[3] cf. F. C. Burkitt, *ERE*, VI.338, 'Gospels', 4(*a*).
[4] cf. McNeile on Matthew 4[13]; also F. W. Green, *St Matthew* (Clarendon Bible), 121.

assisted the Baptist; but the objection of John's disciples seems decisive against this. So 4⁴⁵ may refer to a time later than the Passover, and Jesus may have completed His first Judaean ministry with a second visit to Jerusalem in connexion with, say, Pentecost—a visit not otherwise noticed in any Gospel. Such a course of events would leave time between 3²⁴ and 4²³ (=Mark 1¹⁴) for the arrest of the Baptist. M. Dods[5] suggests that 'he began to do these things' (5¹⁶) shows that other sabbath healings had occurred. Similarly, 'all the things which he did' (4⁴⁵) appears to indicate that healings had taken place other than that of the infirm man at Bethesda; indeed, it might seem not to include that occurrence, since no one knew of it at the time except Jesus and the man himself, and at least one disciple who transmitted the account. 'The Galileans' did not 'see' this 'thing'. John in 4⁵⁴ may be silently elaborating Mark's statement (1¹⁴), and indicating that the Healing of the Officer's Son occurred before the call of the four disciples related in Mark 1¹⁶ff.

The 'officer's son' seems to be the same person as the 'centurion's servant' (Matthew 8⁵⁻¹³, Luke 7²⁻¹⁰)[6]. H. F. D. Sparks[7] holds that John was probably right in speaking of a 'son' rather than a 'servant' as do Matthew and Luke. In Proto-Luke (the Markan sections being omitted) no individual healing is mentioned before this,[8] although there is a statement that, immediately before the Sermon, a multitude came and were healed. In Matthew also there is a general statement that 'Jesus went about all Galilee . . . healing . . .' (4²³⁻⁵), but the first individual healing is that of the leper, followed by that of the centurion's servant, while the healing of Peter's wife's mother and

[5] *EGT.*
[6] cf. B. W. Bacon, *DCG*, II.48a; also *FGH*, 17, and *SFG*, 162.
[7] *JTS*, XLII.179–80.
[8] cf. V. Taylor's *First Draft of St Luke's Gospel.*

those at eventide come later, in agreement with John as
here rearranged. The incident is not recorded by Mark,
although the healing of the leper is mentioned as the
principal feature of the first preaching tour of Jesus when
accompanied by four disciples (Mark 1[40-5]). Thus it seems
to belong to the very beginning of the ministry in Galilee.
Edersheim[9] places the healing of the officer's son immediately before the (Lucan) visit to Nazareth. A. E.
Garvie[10] suggests that Mark 1[14] continues the story of
4[54], as does F. J. Brown.[11]

Taking all the records together it would appear that
Peter was not always in the company of Jesus in the early
days.[12] W. F. Howard[13] says that, early in Galilee, there
was 'not yet a chosen band of twelve, but a more loosely
attached company of followers, amongst whom Peter . . .
was not yet to be counted'. In Mark 1[16] we find him
following his avocation of fisherman, and in Luke 5[1-3] he
is busy washing his nets whilst Jesus is teaching the people
close by. If John is right in placing the healing of the
officer's son immediately on Jesus' return from Judaea,
then it was before Peter was invited to discipleship: consequently his silence on the matter (in Mark) is due to
his absence on that occasion. Mark 3[14]—'that they might
be with him'—indicates that they (Peter and some others)
had not hitherto been with Him continuously.

This incident as narrated by John is often included
amongst those said to be allegorical. Von Hügel[14] says
that John has 'transformed' this story 'almost beyond
recognition'. On the contrary, the fact is that it is John
who enables us to see what really happened; and it is
clear that he intends no allegory, but plain narrative. He
shows that the officer was not a Roman centurion, but

[9] *Life and Times of Jesus the Messiah*, I.x.   [10] *GBD*, 56.
[11] *ET*, LVII.218.   [12] *BJ*, 129; and C. A. Briggs, *ET*, XV.68.
[13] *AC*, 123.   [14] *EBr*.XIV.

served under Herod.[15]   J. Gardner-Smith[16] asks, '. . . what was a Roman officer doing in the dominions of Antipas? John's *basilikos* is more likely to be original.' C. Gore[17] says: 'Herod had his own army and collected his own revenue.'   John also gives the reply of Jesus to the Jewish elders, whom Luke alone says were present, but corrects the impression left by Luke's account that the officer himself did not approach Jesus. The officer had asked his friends to intercede for him, which they did, and so it was to them that Jesus replied: 'Except you (*plural*) see signs. . . .' Then the officer,[18] fearing that his request was not to be granted, made his own appeal: 'Sir, come down before my boy dies'; and Jesus replied: 'I will come and heal him' (Matthew 8[7]), and 'started to go (*eporeueto*, Luke 7[6]) with them.' John further shows that the supposition that Jesus 'entered Capernaum' was mistaken, as the incident occurred at Cana. A. H. McNeile,[19] on Matthew 8[5], suggests that the reading of the Old Latin *k* and the *Sinaitic* Syriac MS.— 'After these things', instead of 'Now when he had entered into Capernaum'—may represent the true text: in which case no evangelist says that Jesus was in Capernaum at this time, since Luke 7[1] appears to belong to what goes before rather than to what follows. But a journey toward Capernaum is begun, during which the officer thinks of the time it will take to travel all those twenty miles— the 'elders' naturally being unable to travel quickly—and then of the well-known Jewish prejudice against entering a Gentile dwelling, and is led to wonder whether Jesus will enter the house or merely stand outside and speak words of healing. But if a word is enough it can be spoken twenty miles away as usefully as twenty cubits. So again

---

[15] J. G. Tasker, *DCG*, II.247b.   [16] *G-S*, 22n.   [17] *Jesus of Nazareth*, 27.
[18] cf. J. Estlin Carpenter, *The Johannine Writings*, 381.
[19] *The Gospel according to Matthew*. Also *FGG*, 276.

D

he says to Jesus: 'Sir, do not trouble yourself . . . say the word, and let my boy be healed; for I myself. . . .' Jesus marvels at the man's insight and says: 'I have not found such great faith, no, not in Israel.'

In the Synoptic contexts this sounds somewhat extravagant, and it is sometimes suggested that the incident cannot belong to the early ministry, since 'Israel' has not yet had any reasonable opportunity to exercise faith. But our rearrangement appears to vindicate itself in the context —probably felt by the evangelist—on the one hand, of the disappointment of Jesus with Israel as represented by Jerusalem and Judaea (§§ 2–4), which had been given the opportunity of accepting Him and His message and had rejected it, with the consequence that He 'forsook Judaea and went into Galilee'; and on the other hand, of the quick understanding faith of this (probably Gentile) officer.

T. W. Manson[20] notes that whilst Luke and Matthew agree verbally in most of the officer's words and in Jesus' reply, as though both were using the same written source, the narrative portion is given differently as though the other details were not certainly known. John as usual does not repeat what the Synoptists have said, except so far as is necessary to his own story. He tells us that Jesus assures the man that his son is alive (and will live); then apparently allows the officer and his friends to continue their journey home, but Himself turns back and goes to Nazareth. These points seem strongly to favour an eye-witness. Both Matthew and John appear to support Luke's date for the visit to Nazareth; and 'the things done in Capernaum' (Luke 4²³) seem to support John. Jesus' references to the widow of Zarephath and to Naaman may have been chosen because the officer was a Gentile: he believed whilst Jesus' own

[20] *The Teaching of Jesus*, 30.

people did not. That the man was a Gentile may have been the point of difference between Jesus and the people of Nazareth.[21]

SECTION 6

6[1]–7[14].—That ch. 6 should follow ch. 4 is generally admitted. Moffatt[1] notes that 'the connexion of 4[54] and 6[1] is certainly good', although he leaves ch. 5 in its traditional position between them. When ch. 5 is taken out it is sometimes urged that since the officer's son has been healed at Capernaum it is natural to say that 'Jesus went away across the Sea of Galilee'. But this overlooks the fact that the whole of the Galilean ministry comes between these two points, and that John has deliberately omitted it. The healing took place just as that ministry was about to begin, while the feeding occurred at the end. Note further that whereas 4[54] speaks of the healing as 'a second sign', in 6[2 ff.] the crowd follow Him 'because they beheld the signs which he kept doing . . .'. This does not accord with a journey across the lake being taken immediately after the healing, but it does accord with the many healings of the Galilean ministry then drawing to its close. Besides, Jesus was not in Capernaum, but at or near Cana.

Again it is often suggested that 6[1], 'After these things he went off across the Sea of Galilee', does not fit in after 5[47], where Jesus is in Jerusalem, so ch. 5 (with 7[15-24]) is put between chh. 6 and 7. But in 7[24] Jesus is still in Jerusalem, and then it is said (7[1]) that He 'walked in Galilee . . .', which is just as unfitting as the former

[21] cf. *CLJ*, 153.   [1] *ILNT*, 554.

sequence, and would seem to require some such intermediate statement as that He 'left Jerusalem and went
into Galilee'. When, however, we take into account the
imperfect tense of 7[1] and correctly render it, 'Jesus continued to go about in Galilee . . .', where He was already
(6[71]), the sequence is quite satisfactory and needs no
alteration. That 'Jesus would not go about in Judaea
. . .' seems to be stated as the reason why He did not
attend the Passover mentioned as imminent at 6[4]. It
may have been exceptional for Him not to attend at
least the prescribed festivals; and this Passover and the
following Pentecost when He was on His northern itinerary
were perhaps the only ones not attended.

But as appears from the Synoptic narrative, His regular
ministry in Capernaum is concluded, and His 'going about'
is more or less furtive in character (see Mark 7[24], 9[30])—
His endeavour being to bring His disciples to an understanding of Himself and His message while warding off
His enemies. He is convinced, especially after the events
mentioned in ch. 6, that further public work in that neighbourhood will not promote the ends He seeks; but He
still needs to complete the training of the Twelve.[2] Mark
gives the outline of this going about in his chh. 7–9 (omit-
ting 8[1-10] at least, as a duplication of 6[32-44], etc.). John,
in 7[1], confirms Mark's order, perhaps designedly.

The 'seeking to kill him' of 5[18] and 7[19] was the likely
result of Jesus' breaking of the sabbath tradition and
claiming special relationship with God. If He had ceased
to do such things nothing more might have been heard
of it; and in fact He retires first to Judaea and then to
Galilee, and the opposition appears to lapse. It revives,
however, later on in Galilee, but there His enemies are
afraid to strike; for He has many sympathizers. But they
mean to lay hold on Him when He goes to Jerusalem,

[2] cf. *GHT*, 102.

which they see He must do if He would establish His claims. In 7¹⁹ the people are not aware of the authorities' desire to kill Him, but in 7²⁵ they are freely talking about it. This presumes a considerable interval of time between the two occasions. When He does go up to the Holy City attempts are made each time to arrest Him, but without success, 'because his hour had not arrived'.

The present arrangement gives an interval of about a year and a half during which no visit to Jerusalem is mentioned, unless at 4⁴⁵, when the interval would still be a year or more. This seems to be confirmed by the expostulation of Jesus' brothers: 'Depart from here and proceed to Judaea, so that your disciples there[3] may behold your works . . . for no one does anything in secret and yet seeks to have himself publicly recognized.' This would not fit any too well if Jesus had been in Jerusalem at the last preceding festival, that of Pentecost, only four months before, as is frequently suggested when ch. 5 is put after ch. 6.

Jesus' statement, 'I am not going up to this feast; for my time has not yet been fulfilled' (7⁸), suggests that He will go up when the season is ripe. 'Now after saying these things he remained in Galilee'—perhaps a week or more. The brothers would go early to 'purify' themselves (cf. 11⁵⁵) and would travel slowly with the great company of pilgrims.[4] The 'ritual of purification might last a whole week'[5] (cf. Acts 21²⁴, ²⁷). Later, under divine direction, Jesus went up, no doubt quickly, perhaps through Samaria (Luke 9⁵²),[6] and even then 'the feast was already half over' when 'he went up to the Temple'. After Peter's confession Jesus envisages His 'exodus' (Luke 9³¹). He now knows He can 'draw all men' to Himself; for He has won Simon Peter: so at length He goes to

---

[3] Reading *ekei* for *kai*.   [4] Edersheim, *Jesus the Messiah*, 294.
[5] *BJ*, 408.   [6] *GHT*, 96–7.

Jerusalem and puts forth His claims. He had been a long time absent from the Metropolis, and now came up having definite knowledge of His enemies' intentions, so that He carefully surveyed the situation before He made any decided move. For a day or two He taught quietly; then, when sure of His ground, He made a decided stand, as narrated in §§ 7–13.

SECTIONS 7, 8, 9 AND 10

7¹⁴ ... Jesus went up to the Temple and began to teach.

²⁵ So some of the Jerusalemites began to say, Is not this he whom they seek to kill?

²⁶ And see, he is speaking openly, and yet they are saying nothing to him. Can it be that the rulers really know that this is the Christ?

²⁷ No, we know where this man is from, but the Christ, whenever he comes—no one will know where he is from.

²⁸ So, while teaching in the Temple, Jesus cried aloud, saying, You both know me and know where I am from. And yet I have not come on my own authority, but he that sent me is real, whom you do not know.

²⁹ I know him; for I am from him and he commissioned me.

⁴⁰ So some of the crowd, when they heard these words, said, Truly this is the Prophet.

⁴¹ Others said, This is the Christ. But some said, What, does the Christ come out of Galilee?

⁴² Has not the scripture said, Of the seed of David and from Bethlehem—the village where David was —*comes* the Christ?

⁴³   There arose therefore a division among the crowd on his account.

³⁰   So they were wanting to arrest him, and yet no one laid his hand on him, because his hour had not yet come.

³¹   But many of the crowd believed in him and said, When the Christ does come will he do more signs than this man has done?

³²   The Pharisees heard the crowd murmuring these things about him, and so the high priests and the Pharisees dispatched guards to arrest him;

⁴⁴   and some of them wished to arrest him, but no one laid hands on him.

⁴⁵   So the guards came to the high priests and Pharisees and they said to them, Why did you not bring him?

⁴⁶   The guards answered, No man ever spoke thus.

7²⁵⁻⁹.—With 7¹⁵⁻²⁴ taken out to follow ch. 5, this section follows 7¹⁴, and the result seems quite satisfactory. This sequence is generally recognized. Compare the following:

7¹   The Jews were seeking to kill Him.
7   The world . . . hates Me.
²⁵   Is not this He whom they want to kill?

7⁴⁰⁻³.—Verses 40–2 seem to belong to the same occasion as vv. 26–7.

7³⁰⁻².—Verse 30 appears to follow well on v. 43, and v. 31 to follow naturally on vv. 26–7 and 40–2. Verse 31 is a summary of the situation as regards the crowd, while v. 32 begins a fresh paragraph respecting the official attitude.

7⁴⁴⁻⁵².—Several writers propose to put 7⁴⁵⁻⁵² before 7³⁷⁻⁴⁴ so as to bring the guards' report of their non-arrest of Jesus on the same day as the arrest was ordered. The present arrangement effects this even more closely. The traditional sequence appears to mean that some of 'the crowd' (v. 43) 'wished to arrest him' (v. 44). But this is very unlikely, as is shown by v. 30, where it is evidently the authorities and their followers who wish to lay their hands on him, since in v. 31 we read, 'But (*alla*, on the contrary) many of the crowd believed in him', and in v. 32 'the high priests . . . dispatched guards to arrest him'. Our arrangement indicates that in v. 44 it was some of the guards who desired it, but not even all of them; for in the end he was not arrested.

Verses 33–6 are transferred to ch. 12 (see §22), and vv. 37–9 become a separate incident, for which see next section.

SECTION 11

7³⁷⁻⁹.—The previous section concludes John's account of Jesus' visit to the festival of the booths, except for the eighth (the last) day, which he now notices. See notes on next section.

SECTION 12

9¹⁻⁴¹.—The feast of Tabernacles had two ceremonies commemorating the Israelites' wanderings in the Wilderness: the carrying of water from Siloam to the Temple, symbolical of 'the water out of the rock'; and the lighting up of the Temple courts as a reminder of 'the pillar

of fire'. The former is referred to in 7³⁷, while ch. 9 offers
a sign suitable to the latter. Hence many seek to bring
in the sign before 7³⁷. But the words, 'Now on the last
day, the great day of the feast', seem to introduce rather
than to conclude that day's happenings as related by
John (see note on previous section). 7³⁷ expressly says
that it was 'on the last day' (and not before) that Jesus
made His reference to the water-ceremony. So the lighting-
ceremony also may have been spoken of on the same day.
Indeed, the note of confident exultation in 9³⁻⁵ may indicate that Jesus had been looking for an opportunity of
pointing the moral of the lamps, since it appears that
Jesus himself had 'noticed' the man before the disciples
began to remark on his case; and so He seized with
pleasure on their question about his blindness. There
were, doubtless, several blind men He passed that day,
but not many who had been born blind.

SECTION 13

9³⁹   Jesus said, For judgement came I into this world,
         that those who do not see may begin to see. . . .

40   Some of the Pharisees who were near him . . .
         said to him, Are we also blind?

41   Jesus said, . . . your sin remains.

8¹²   Jesus therefore spoke to them again and said,
         I am the light of the world . . .

8¹²⁻²⁰.—This section is eminently suitable as a discourse
accompanying the sign of ch. 9 (cf. 9⁵, ³⁹, ⁴⁰, 8¹²), and as
the discourse on the event could hardly come before the
event itself, it would appear that 8¹²⁻²⁰ should follow 9⁴¹.

A. C. Headlam[1] connects these two sections. At any rate, that 8[20] states that the words were spoken in the Treasury (near the Women's Court where the golden lamps were lit during the festival)[2] agrees well with our arrangement. C. Clare Oke[3] suggests that 8[12ff.] should follow ch. 9, but with 10[19-21] between. 8[12-20] is sometimes read after 7[52] (7[53]–8[11]) omitted, but it does not suitably follow it.[4] In the narrative of the meeting of the high priests and Pharisees there is nothing to account for 'therefore', 'again', or 'them' (8[12]), since Jesus was not present at their meeting. Bernard, while following this order, recognizes that the sequence is neither easy nor sure. Nor does it fit in after 7[15-24], where some writers place it; for it deals with a theme entirely absent from 5[1-47], 7[15-24]. But 9[39-41] supplies exactly the right sequence: 'I am the light of the world' comes well after 'I came . . . that those who do not see may begin to see'. Compare also the more remote 'When I am in the world I am the Light of the world' (9[5]), which, being limited in scope—'While I am in the world'—cannot come after the universal of 8[12]: it would then be a kind of bathos.[5]

J. A. Robertson[6] favours the placing of 8[12-20] after 9[41], as does J. A. Findlay.[7] Bernard also appears to approve the connexion of 8[12-20] with the feast of Tabernacles, and notes the parallel of 8[12] and 9[5]: 'I am the light of the world.'[8] Whatever its connexion, this section is obviously not the beginning but the continuation of an address by Jesus which in some way has been interrupted. The word 'therefore (oun)' is not used when continuing the record of a speech, although Jesus had been speaking in 9[41]. But it is sometimes used to resume after an interruption,[9] and

[1] FGH, 10.   [2] cf. HDB, I.861b.   [3] ET, XLVII.425-7.
[4] J. M. Thompson in Exp, VIII.ix.423; also F. W. Lewis, Disarrangements, 17.
[5] cf. BJ, in loc.   [6] Study Bible.
[7] The Way, the Truth, and the Life, 266.
[8] BJ, 291-2.   [9] Grim-Thayer, s.v. (§ c).

it may be so here: Jesus had been, almost certainly, addressing persons other than the Pharisees before their intervention, 'therefore' turns to 'them' 'again' after dealing with the interrupters. But these latter continue to ask questions, and the rest of this section gives His reply.

SECTION 14

10¹⁹⁻²⁹.—Verse 21 clearly refers to ch. 9. Then 10¹⁹, 'a division *again* occurred among the Jews', agrees with 9¹⁶, 'There was a division among them [i.e. the Pharisees]',[1] whilst 8¹³⁻¹⁹ deals wholly with the Pharisees' disputation with Jesus. Some of them evidently were impressed with His real power, hence the 'division among them'.

Westcott[2] notes that 10¹⁹ has no historical connexion with its preceding context. This section is frequently placed before 10¹⁻¹⁸, and this order seems to connect up the sayings about the 'sheep' and the 'sheep-fold' much better than does the traditional order, which divides the discourse into two parts, seemingly delivered on different occasions.

SECTION 15

10¹⁻¹⁸.—Jesus appears to use the asseveration, 'Truly, truly, I tell you', only in reference to some theme already under consideration. There is nothing in ch. 9 to account for it at 10¹; but it follows well on 10²⁷⁻⁹. Note the following parallels:

[1] *BJ*, 341.   [2] *WJ*, Intro. II.6.1.

10²⁷ The sheep which are mine listen to my voice, and
        I know them, and they follow me.

  4   The sheep follow him, because they know his voice.

 14   I know them that are mine.

 28   I give them eternal life.

 10   I am come that they may have life.

SECTION 16

10³⁰–12¹⁹.—See the note on §15 for this order.

Before Jesus' last Passover definite instructions were
issued by the Jewish authorities that, whenever He should
again enter the Capital, any one who knew His whereabouts must reveal it; for the decision had been taken
(11⁴⁷⁻⁵³) to put Him to death. This decision He meets
openly: first, by coming without concealment to Bethany;
then by His own challenge of the Triumphal Entry.

SECTION 17

12¹⁹   So the Pharisees
        said one to another, 'You perceive that you are
        effecting nothing, See, the world has gone after him.'

7⁵³   And they went every one to his own house; but Jesus
8¹   went to the Hill of the Olives.

  2   And at dawn he set out[1] again for the Temple.

  3   And the scribes and Pharisees bring to him a
        woman . . .

---

[1] Reading the *imperfect, paregineto,* not used again in the New Testament except at 3²³.

7⁵³–8¹¹.—We omit the words placed in square brackets by Hort and Nestle.

As is well known this section is not found in any of the most ancient uncials except D; no early Greek-speaking commentator whose work has survived mentions it;[2] and it is absent from several good cursive manuscripts. It is also agreed that in language and grammatical usage it differs considerably from the rest of John. On the other hand it is found in D, in some early Latin texts, in Jerome's Vulgate, and in most of the later manuscripts, even those which have no affinity with D; so that it must be earlier than the fourth century. Scrivener[3] says: '. . . the text [of D] is in the main identical with one that was current both in the East and in the West as early as the second century of our aera. It may well have been brought into Gaul by Irenaeus . . . about A.D. 170. . . .' Several ancient MSS leave a space indicating that they knew of something found here, which they deliberately omitted.

Perhaps, with all modern editors of the Greek New Testament, we ought to omit these verses. But against this we note that 7⁵³–8¹ forms a fitting conclusion to the story of the Triumphal Entry, and that 8², which begins the main narrative of this section, looks forward to §18 (which see). On the other hand, it cannot follow 7⁵², since Jesus had not been present at the gathering of the high priests and Pharisees.

If it was in the original draft of the Gospel, one outstanding reason for its deliberate omission by the editor is found in the words, 'And Jesus said, Neither do I pronounce sentence on you . . .'—meaning, 'I am not an appointed judge;[4] it is not for me to pronounce sentence (cf. 8¹⁵); and since all your accusers are gone, you may

---

2 But cf. *Apostolical Constitutions*, II.24.

3 *Cod. Bezae Cantab.*, xlv.

4 cf. *Ecce Homo*, IV; also *TRJ*, 152.

go, too; but I warn you to turn away from your sin'. With this compare 'Who made me a judge . . .?' (Luke 12[14]).[5] This sense of the words was early obscured; and obviously they are open to the careless interpretation, 'I do not want to be hard on you: off you go!', an interpretation common from early times to the present day.

In view of this and of the urgent need of raising and not lowering the moral tone amongst Gentile believers, the responsible person felt justified in withholding this section from publication. This judgement, however, does not apply to quite all the section, since the first two verses belong to a previous incident. If this *pericope* were no part of the Gospel, why should these two verses be included in it?

If, on the other hand, this section was in the original draft—all on one sheet (or two sheets if the writing were on only one side)—then someone decided that it should be suppressed, and possibly noticing that 7[53]–8[1] was not essential to what preceded (especially if, as probably, disarrangement had already occurred), took away the whole section—perhaps it was destroyed. In any case someone who had seen it and remembered its story wrote it out from memory, but in his own words. He may, however, have used some of the original words: *Katalambanein* (overtake, etc.), vv. 3 and 4, for instance, is found in John 1[5], 12[35] (also 6[17] אD), but only once in Mark and not at all in Matthew or Luke. Then *lithazein* (to stone), v. 5, occurs four times in the rest of John, but not in the Synoptics, which use other words having the same meaning; while the injunction, 'Sin no more', is found at 5[14] but not elsewhere in the four Gospels.

If 7[53]–8[1] really does conclude the story of 12[12-19], and if it was written on the same sheet or sheets as 8[2-11], the case for accidental dislocation of this Gospel is strengthened,

[5] cf. *BJ*, 295, 721.

as also for a codex or, more probably, separate sheets in the original draft.

The incident is not said to have occurred in the Temple: at any rate it was not until afterwards that Jesus 'found in the Temple those who were selling . . .' (see next section). So the words, 'set her in the midst', indicate that Jesus was met by the Pharisees somewhere on His way to the Temple (8² — cf. vv. 6, 8: 'on (*eis*) the ground', i.e.: 'in the dust [of the roadway])', and that when He came up to them, along with His disciples, a ring of spectators was formed, and the woman was thrust into the midst before Him.

The story belongs to a late stage in the ministry, when the authorities are anxious to discredit Jesus in the minds of the people on any pretext whatever, as in the Last Week. Westcott says: 'The incident belongs to the last visit to Jerusalem, so that the position it occupies in St Luke [following 21³⁸ in the Ferrar group of manuscripts] is perhaps historically correct.' That the beginning of this section has a verbal parallel in Luke 21, and that the style and vocabulary resemble what is found in the Third Gospel, have led a number of scholars to suggest that originally it belonged there. But its textual history shows that it is much more remote from Luke than from John, being found in Luke only in a few cursives, which is no sign of antiquity, but only of the exercise of criticism. On the other hand a much earlier criticism worked in the opposite direction, and consequently D interpolates in v. 2 (apparently from Luke 21³⁸), 'and all the people came to him'. The further statement, found in many authorities, 'and he sat down and taught them', is a natural addition. These addenda, however, interrupt and give a false turn to the narrative, in which, as noted above, Jesus does not arrive at the Temple until after the end of the present section.

There is nothing in 12[12-19] to suggest that the Triumphal Entry took place late in the day. Mark 11[11], however, says that, following the procession to the city, 'He entered into Jerusalem, into the Temple, and when he had carefully observed everything that was going on, it being already evening, he went out to Bethany with the Twelve'. John 8[1] agrees with the latter part of this statement, and even better with Luke 21[37]: 'At night he went out and lodged in the Hill called the Olive-orchard' (see also 22[39]). 'The Hill of the Olives' (John 8[1]) may be more correct than 'Bethany' (Mark 11[11-12]), at any rate Mark 11[19] does not mention Bethany, but says that 'when evening came [after the Cleansing] they (he) went outside the city'. Perhaps the fact is that He was at Bethany on the night before the Triumphal Entry, but after that event went to Olivet (which probably means Gethsemane—cf. John 18[1-2]). Martha's house may have been watched by spies (cf. Mark 14[1], Luke 19[47-8], John 12[10-11]), and Jesus may have lodged elsewhere with the deliberate intention of averting danger from the family at Bethany as well as settling the location where Judas would ultimately find Him on the night of the betrayal. If Mark's 'Bethany' were correct how did it happen that Jesus escaped from Martha's house 'hungry' (Mark 11[12])? John 12[36] says that Jesus 'went away and hid from them'. Where did He go? The house at Bethany was well known.[6] Is not Gethsemane[7] the likeliest place?[8]

John 12[12-19], 7[53]–8[11], 2[13b-22], are in exactly the same order as Mark 11[1-19], except that the latter has nothing of John 8[3-11], but inserts the incident (or parable) of the Barren Fig-tree; while 8[1-2] is definitely supported in the same historical sequence by Mark 11[11, 12, 19]. Further, we learn from Mark that the Cleansing occurred, not on

---

[6] cf. F. Mauriac, *Life of Jesus*, 212.   [7] cf. *G-S*, 56–7.
[8] cf. A. C. Deane, *Jesus Christ*, 110–11.

the day of the Triumphal Entry, but on the day following. F. C. Burkitt[9] looks on the separation by Mark of
the Cleansing from the Entry as a real historical reminis-
cence: neither Luke nor Matthew mentions it. If we put
2[13b-22] immediately after 12[19] there is nothing to show
that these events did not occur consecutively on the same
day. But John is careful to note times and places; and
7[53]-8[2] supplies what is here required. The sequence of
events is indicated thus: the Triumphal Entry (late in
the day, Mark 11[11]); the retirement for the night of the
Pharisees (7[53]) and of Jesus (8[1], Mark 11[11]); Jesus' return
next morning (8[2], Mark 11[12]) to the Temple; and its
Cleansing (2[13b-22], Mark 11[15-18]).

In view of all these considerations this section is placed
after 12[19] and before 2[13b].

SECTION 18

8[2]	And at dawn he set out again for the Temple.
3	And the scribes and Pharisees bring to him a woman . . .
11	And Jesus said, '. . . go, from this time sin no more.'
2[13b]	And Jesus went up to Jerusalem,
14	and found in the Temple those who were selling . . .

2[13b-25].—John often repeats his statements in a different
form, and in 13b may be completing 8[2]. For the phrase-
ology cf. Mark 11[15]: 'And he came to Jerusalem, and
when he had entered into the Temple. . . .'

Since in the traditional order the Cleansing of the Temple
is found at the beginning of the ministry, some have

[9] Art. 'Gospels', *ERE*, VI.339.

E

supposed that such an act was performed twice, whilst many accept John's order of events as against Mark's. But the present arrangement completely removes the difficulty, as now the event is placed in exactly the same position in all four Gospels. Moreover, John's account gives a reason in v. 19 for the charge made against Jesus (Mark 14[58]) of which we have no explanation elsewhere.[1]

Jesus did not anywhere begin with violence, but with persuasion, however firm He was in declaring His attitude to things.[2] That this is so seems certain when we remember how bitterly disappointed He was that the right response to His message failed to appear: 'Woe to thee, Chorazin . . .' (Luke 10[13-15]); 'O Jerusalem . . . that killest the prophets . . .' (Luke 13[34-5]); 'He saw the city and wept over it . . .' (Luke 19[41-4]).[3] To have performed such an act as the Cleansing at the beginning of His ministry would have been Himself to raise opposition to His message, whereas the opposition always sprang from others—compare His attitude to sabbath observance. But things being as they were, an outward protest against the practices of the Annas clique could hardly be avoided, although Jesus knew perfectly well what it would mean, so that it was fittingly reserved until the time when there was no longer any hope of His acceptance by the authorities as representing the nation. For an unknown person to have attempted such a deed would have been useless: no one, money-changers, drovers or priests would have paid any heed to Him; and the Temple guards would quickly have arrested Him or put Him outside.[4] The act was possible only because everybody knew who He was and knew His favour with the crowds of pilgrims,

[1] *ANT*, 353.
[2] cf. *CHE*, 419.
[3] C. J. Cadoux, *Historic Mission of Jesus*, 18, 183–93; *CLJ*, 79–81; also R. Dunkerley in *ET*, LVIII.133ff., 161ff.
[4] *MJ*, xiv.

who in their thousands had cheered Him through the
streets the day before: 'they were afraid of him; for all
the crowd was astonished at his teaching' (Mark 11[18]).
See also Luke 19[47-8], 20[19], 22[2].[5] It would not have availed
the authorities to order His arrest: that had been tried
six months earlier (7[32]), and the guards had come back
without Him. This latter occurrence could not have happened if Jesus were known to be a disturber of the peace,
i.e. if the Cleansing had taken place at the beginning of
the ministry. Hence they were helpless, as had been the
Pharisees the evening before, when they confessed: 'The
world has gone after him.'

The incident must have occurred toward the end of the
ministry:[6] otherwise, what we must suppose was deemed
by the authorities to be a grave offence (Mark 15[29]) was
overlooked for two years, and remembered (Mark 14[58])
only when Jesus was arrested on another charge. Bernard
says:[7] 'On psychological grounds, the incident is hardly
credible, if it is to be put at the beginning of the ministry
of Jesus . . . we find it difficult to suppose that . . . anything like it could have happened at so early a stage. . . .'
Schmiedel asks:[8] 'Is it conceivable that, after driving the
dealers from the forecourt of the Temple, and supposing
that it took place at the beginning of the visits to Jerusalem, He could have continued to work for two years
unmolested?' W. F. Howard writes:[9] '. . . the reforming
zeal that swept the money-changers from the courts was
too bold a challenge to vested interests to escape swift
and effective retribution.' On the other hand, the fact
that in 5[12-15] Jesus is unknown to the infirm man, to the
crowd and to the Jews, who ask, 'Who is he . . .?', makes
it almost unthinkable that the Temple Cleansing had
already happened. Whenever ch. 5 is dated it cannot

---

[5] cf. A. C. Deane, *Jesus Christ*, 106.   [6] *FGH*, 3.   [7] *BJ*, 88–9.
[8] *The Johannine Writings*, 72.   [9] *LQHR*, January 1942.

follow 2[13b-22], since Jesus must have been thereafter a marked man to the authorities and their supporters.

Some writers suggest that, whilst the Synoptics regarded the Cleansing as the act of provocation which precipitated Jesus' death, John appears to think that the Raising of Lazarus was the real cause. But our rearrangement makes this distinction unnecessary.[10] Indeed, that Jesus knew that the Sadducean party had reached the point of explosion on account of the Raising of Lazarus (12[9-11]; Luke 19[37]: 'the whole multitude of the disciples began to rejoice and to praise God with a loud voice for all the mighty works which they had seen'), may well have been His opportunity for the Cleansing. J. Gardner-Smith[11] writes: 'In the Synoptic Gospels the Cleansing of the Temple is placed during the last week before the crucifixion, and the resentment of the Sadducean authorities accounts in large measure for the arrest of Jesus. But their resentment applies to the Raising of Lazarus also.' A. E. Brooke[12] asks: '. . . is not something more needed to explain the Markan narrative of the Triumphal Entry than is found in St Mark?' Although the Sanhedrin had agreed to have Jesus put to death (11[53]) and had given orders that any person knowing His whereabouts must give information (11[57]), yet the Triumphal Entry, which all too clearly revealed His whereabouts, had also shown how strongly the popular feeling was in His favour, so that the Pharisees at least were puzzled to know what to do. The authorities would have been unable to fulfil their purpose, and Jesus would have been free to leave Jerusalem at the end of the festival, apart from His own action: first, by the Cleansing of the Temple, which revived the fierceness of their opposition, and, finally, the dismissal of Judas from His company in the Upper Room. Jesus knew that His action in the Cleansing would bring

[10] cf. *FGH*, 39–40.   [11] *G-S*, 13.   [12] *CBE*, 314.

the enmity of the rulers to a head, and that it would have the effect of averting from Lazarus the hostility of the high priests (12¹⁰). With this compare His care for the disciples' safety in the garden (18⁸). The Cleansing seems to have occurred on the day appointed (10 Nisan) for the selection of the Paschal lamb, i.e. just when the market was at its busiest. By His act Jesus offered Himself, and was accepted by the authorities on behalf of the nation, as the true Paschal Lamb (cf. Exodus 12³⁻⁶).

Mark 11²⁸ places the question of John 2¹⁸ on the day following the Cleansing. Luke 20¹ says: 'On one of the days.' The only other request of the authorities for a sign is mentioned by Mark (8¹¹) after the Feeding of the Four Thousand (cf. John 6³⁰), while Luke (11¹⁶, ²⁹ ff.) connects it with the Beelzebub controversy, and Matthew inserts it in both places. None of them puts it early in the ministry. In any case, the question does not seem appropriate to the first contact of Jesus with the authorities, as at John 2¹⁸ in its traditional position, since it presupposes that He is already an established teacher. Bernard (xxx *n.*) suggests that the question would not be suitable after the Raising of Lazarus. But the Sadducees, who did not believe in any resurrection, would not accept that event as a fact any more than they accepted the resurrection of Jesus Himself. If they had believed that Lazarus had come back from the dead they might have accepted the claims of Jesus. 'Neither will they believe if one rise from the dead!'

2¹⁹, interpreted by vv. 21–2, seems to be thought of as referring to Jesus' death. No other such reference, except that of 'the bridegroom' being taken away (Mark 2²⁰—possibly not in chronological order) appears in any Gospel before about the time of Peter's confession. That the words, 'Destroy this sanctuary, and within three days

I will raise it up', are taken by John to refer to the Crucifixion and the Resurrection, would seem to indicate that
they were spoken not long before those events, especially
as a garbled account of them was brought forward at
the Trial.

'Forty-six years' (2[20]) is generally supposed to bring
down the date of the Cleansing to A.D. 27, as by Turner[13]
and others, or to A.D. 28. P. W. Schmiedel[14] says that
this Passover 'will be, if the forty-sixth year was not yet
ended, that of A.D. 27; if it was ended, which suits the
expression better, that of A.D. 28. Josephus[15] says that
in his eighteenth year Herod 'undertook . . . to build . . .
the Temple'. He announced his intention, and then 'told
them he would not pull down the Temple till all things
were got ready for building it up again. And . . . he did
not break his word', but brought great stores, and trained
masons and carpenters for the work, 'and then began to
build; but this not till everything was well prepared for
the work'. This last statement seems to put the actual
start of the building to a time later than Herod's eighteenth
year by perhaps one or even two years; so that it is not
unlikely that the date of John 2[20] is A.D. 29, i.e. the probable year of the Crucifixion.

SECTION 19

2[23]　　Now when he was in Jerusalem at the Passover,
　　　during the feast, many believed in his name, behold-
　　　ing his signs which he was doing;

[24]　　but Jesus on his part would not trust himself to
　　　them; for that he knew all men,

[13] *HDB*.　　[14] *EB*, 2542.　　[15] *Ant*. XV.XI.I (Whiston's Translation).

25   and because he had no need that any one should
testify concerning man; for he himself knew what
was in man.

8³¹   Jesus, therefore, began to say to the Jews who
had believed him, If you continue in my word you
are really my disciples;

32   and you will understand the truth, and the truth
will set you free.

8³¹⁻⁵⁹.—The paragraph 2²³⁻⁵ appears to belong to the
later ministry. 'Many believed in his name, beholding
his signs which he kept doing' cannot well belong to the
earliest days, as in the traditional order. At any rate,
we cannot suppose that any disciple then knew his Master
well enough to recognize that 'Jesus would not trust
himself to them . . . for he knew what was in man'.[1]
The paragraph is somewhat bare and vague by itself and
seems to need something to substantiate it. 8³¹⁻⁵⁹ is
suitable as the illustrative instance.

This section is obviously the sequel to a statement that
certain persons had begun to exercise toward Jesus some
kind of faith, although not the highest, which John denotes
by the phrase 'to believe *in* him'. It cannot follow 8¹²⁻²⁰
(8²¹⁻³⁰ being taken out), since nothing is there recorded
of belief on the part of anyone; nor can it go along with
8²¹⁻³⁰ (see § 24), for that is required to account for 12³⁴
(see § 25); hence it is left isolated, since it has no connexion
with ch. 9, which follows it in the traditional order. We
note, however, that some scribe appears to have tried to
connect the two chapters by adding to ch. 8 the words,
'and going through the midst of them went his way, and
so passed by'; which he no doubt meant should match
the words, 'And as he passed by', which begin ch. 9.

There does not seem to be any connexion with any

[1] cf. Greville P. Lewis in *ET*, XLIV.228ff.

section whatever if not with 2²³⁻⁵. The Nicodemus incident is sometimes thought to be suitably introduced by the latter, but 8³¹ff. would appear to be even more appropriate, whilst 3¹ff. follows immediately on that. John 2²³⁻⁵, the faith of those who 'believed in his name, beholding his signs', is shown to be of a secondary kind by the fact that 'Jesus would not trust himself to them'. Bernard[2] says: 'Their belief was neither stable nor adequate' (cf. 6²). The faith of those who 'believed him' (8³¹) would appear also to be of this secondary nature. So Jesus proceeds to test their faith and to show up its deficiency.

If this section does come later in the narrative than 10³¹, the word 'again' found there will probably require deletion, since 8⁵⁹ would then follow instead of preceding it. The word is omitted from D, some Latin copies, etc.

SECTION 20

3¹⁻¹³.—That the interview with Nicodemus is to be placed at the end of the ministry, as by Tatian in the *Diatessaron*, is accepted by many. Nicodemus mentions 'these signs which you are doing', although no public sign has yet been noted in the traditional order, except the general statement of 2²³ (see the two preceding sections). Then, why should Nicodemus come by night unless Jesus was under suspicion of the authorities? But there is no suggestion of this in chh. 1 or 2 except the Cleansing: in the earlier ministry as recorded in the Synoptics the scribes used to sit in public places listening to Jesus (Mark 2⁶, etc.). Hence it would appear that this incident must be placed in the Last Week along with the Cleansing.[1]

---

[2] *BJ*, 98.   [1] cf. E. B. Redlich in *ET*, LV.89–92.

Moreover, we have here the mention by Jesus of 'the Spirit'. Except in the Last Discourses this is the only occasion recorded by John when Jesus Himself speaks of the personal Spirit. In Mark the first promise of the Holy Spirit to the disciples is given only when Jesus has left the Temple for the last time (Mark 13[11]).[2] According to John, the Spirit was referred to at the feast of Booths under the symbol of 'living water', but was not named by Jesus. Here, however, he is definitely introduced as a Person who 'breathes where he wills' (cf. 1 Corinthians 12[11]).[3] The next mention is at 14[16-17], where Jesus, in view of His own speedy departure, promises that 'the Father will send you another advocate, that he may be with you for ever . . .'; then follows 15[25], where the nature of the Spirit is indicated as one 'proceeding from the Father'; next comes 16[7-14], where His work is explained in relation to the world and also to the disciples; and, finally, at 14[26], for the first and only time, Jesus gives His full designation: 'The Holy Spirit.' See notes on §§ 30, 32, and 35 for this order. All this tends to confirm the view that this incident occurred only shortly before the end.

SECTION 21

3[11]   We . . . testify to what we have seen, and our
         testimony you do not accept . . .

13   And no one has ascended up to heaven except
         he that descended out of heaven. The Son of man,

31   who comes from above, is above all . . . He that
32   comes out of heaven testifies to what he has seen
         and heard, and his testimony no one accepts.

[2] cf. *XJ*, 78.   [3] cf. C. J. Wright, *Jesus the Revelation of God*, 131–2.

3[31-6]—In this section we omit the words in vv. 31-2 which are omitted in the above text. J. H. Michael[1] has this sequence, which Macgregor follows. That there is some break in the sense between vv. 13 and 16 is felt by many. V. Burch[2] places 3[31-6] after 3[15]. Cadoux[3] exchanges 3[22-30] and 3[31-6]. In the present rearrangement 3[14-21] follows 12[36a] (see §26). That 3[31-1] rightly follows 3[1-13] is supported by the repetition of ideas, as follows:

3[2]   You have come from God.
[34]   He whom God sent.

[3]   [The once-born] cannot see the Kingdom of God.
[6]   That which is begotten of the flesh is flesh.
[31] He that is of the earth . . . speaks of the earth.

[11] We . . . testify to what we have seen, and our testimony you do not accept.
[32] He . . . testifies to what he has seen and heard, and his testimony no one accepts.

[13] He that descended out of heaven.
[31] Who comes down out of heaven . . . He that comes out of heaven.

That these two sections belong to the close of the ministry is confirmed by the statements, 'You (*plural*) do not accept our testimony' and 'His testimony no one accepts', which, especially the latter, are too sweeping to be suitable to an early visit of Jesus to the Holy City. The last phrase of v. 13 is here joined to v. 31. The various readings added to v. 13—'who is in heaven', or 'who is from

[1] *ET*, XXXVII.428-9.   [2] *St John's Gospel*.   [3] *JTS*, July 1919, p. 317.

heaven'—appear to reflect the difficulty caused by the disarrangement of the sections.

Since it obviously differs from the preceding speech of the Baptist (3^{27-30}) as found in the traditional order, and also from the succeeding account of Jesus' withdrawal from Judaea, this small section is often looked on as a comment by the evangelist, as by Von Hügel.[4] But as here arranged it follows perfectly on v. 13, and is an evident part of the interview with Nicodemus. Another alleged ground for regarding it merely as a comment is that it is written in the *third person*; and even as here rearranged something might be said for this opinion, since in 3^{1-12} the answers to Nicodemus are given in the *first* and *second persons*: 'Truly, truly, I tell you . . .' (vv. 3 and 5). We note, however, that a transition to the third person occurs in v. 13, and this form is continued in vv. 31-6.

SECTION 22

12^{20-33}.—Having related how a ruler of the Jews interviewed Jesus, John now mentions that Greek proselytes also sought Him. Verse 33 properly follows the first mention of what it explains. (See below for text.) In v. 32 Jesus says, 'I, if I be lifted up from the earth . . .'; and this is interpreted in v. 33 as indicating the manner of His death. But in v. 34 the crowd asks, 'Who is this Son of man?'—and 'the Son of man' has not been mentioned. 8^{28} is needed—see §25.

[4] *EBr*, XIV.

SECTION 23

12³¹   Now is there a judgement of this world; now
  ³²   shall the ruler of this world be cast out. And I, if
        I be lifted up from the earth, will draw all men
  ³³   to myself. Now this he was saying, signifying by
        what kind of death he was about to die.

7³³   So Jesus said, Yet a little while am I with you,
        and then I go to him that sent me. . . .

7³³⁻⁶.—We note the following correspondences with the
last and the next following sections:

12²³   The hour has come for the Son of man to be
        glorified.
  ²⁷⁻⁸ Shall I say, Father, save me . . .? . . . Father,
        glorify thy name.
  ³²   If I be lifted up from the earth.
  ³³   Signifying by what kind of death he was about
        to die.
7³³⁻⁴ Yet a little while am I with you, and then I go
        to him that sent me. You will seek me and will
        not find me; and where I am you cannot come.
8²¹   I am going away; and you will seek me . . . where
        I am going you cannot come.

'Yet a little while' (7³³) is repeated at 12³⁵ and is found
elsewhere in John (the Greek differently phrased) only at
13³³, 14¹⁹, and 16¹⁶⁻¹⁹. Then, 'I go to him that sent me'
(7³³) occurs again only at 16⁵; 'I go to the Father' is
found at 16¹⁰ ⁽¹⁷⁾; while 'I proceed to the Father' is said
at 14¹², 16²⁸, and 14²⁸. All this suggests that this section
belongs to the very end of the ministry. In v. 35 the
Jews ask, 'Is he about to go . . . and teach the Greeks?'
—perhaps because Greeks were present (12²⁰).

SECTION 24

7³⁶   What is this word which he said, You will seek
        me and . . . where I am you cannot come?

8²¹   Again, therefore, he said to them, I am going
        away, and you will seek me. . . .

8²¹⁻³⁰.—Macgregor puts 8²¹ᶠᶠ· after 7³⁶, but in a different
place in the narrative.[1] Verse 21, like 7³³, appears to be
an explanation of 12³²ᵃ, etc., (see above). Note that this
section begins: 'Again, therefore, *he* said. . . .' If it had
been a separate incident the name 'Jesus' would be
expected. That the statements of 7³⁴ and 8²¹ are directly
referred to in 13³³, 'As I said to the Jews, Where I am
going you cannot come, now I say to you also', suggests
that they had been uttered not long before.

It is possible that 8³⁰ has been added by the editor,
who looked for the antecedent of 8³¹, which, owing to
dislocation, is not found in the traditional context.
Bernard, on this verse, notes that the *genitive absolute* is
infrequent in John. In any case, that v. 31 reads 'believed
him' and not 'believed in him' as at v. 30, suggests that
scribes have been careful to make exact copies of their
exemplars.

SECTION 25

8²⁸   So Jesus said, When you shall have lifted up the
        Son of man, then you will perceive that I am he,
        and that . . . I speak . . . as the Father taught
        me. . . .

[1] cf. *BJ*, 298.

12³⁴   The crowd answered him, We have heard out of the Law that the Christ abides for ever; and how say you, The Son of man must be lifted up? Who is this Son of man?

12³⁴⁻⁶ᵃ.—Verse 34 is better accounted for by 8²⁸ than by 12³², where, as noted by Westcott,[1] the phrase 'the Son of man' does not occur. Moreover, 12³² mentions the person to be 'lifted up'—'I, if I . . .': and the question of v. 34 is inappropriate if it is to follow immediately. Some rearrangement seems to be required. The query, as often with Jesus, is not answered at once, but a warning, similar to that of 12³⁰⁻¹, is uttered, and a reply to the question only comes later in 3¹⁴⁻¹⁵ (for which see next section). In the traditional order the people's question remains unanswered. H. B. Swete[2] connects 12³⁶ with 8²¹ in interpretation. F. R. Hoare[3] puts 12³⁴ff. into the middle of 8²⁸.

SECTION 26

12³⁵   So Jesus said to them, Yet a little while is the light among you. Walk while you have the light, lest darkness overtake you.

36   . . . while you have the light believe in the light, that you may become sons of light.

3¹⁴   And yet, just as Moses lifted up the serpent in the wilderness, so must the Son of man be lifted

19   up . . . light has come into the world and they loved darkness rather than light. . . .

3¹⁴⁻²¹.—Macgregor brings this section into ch. 12, but breaks it up and arranges it differently: 12³², 3¹⁴, ¹⁵, 12³⁴,

[1] *WJ*, Intro. II.6.i.   [2] *Last Discourses and Prayer of Jesus*, xiv.n.
[3] See *ET*, LVII.217–20.

3¹⁶⁻²¹, with 12³³ omitted as a gloss. P. G. Lewis[1] has the same order except that 3¹², ¹³ precedes 3¹⁶⁻²¹. We note that 3¹⁴, a renewed affirmation of the 'lifting up', is an appropriate answer to 12³⁴,[2] and that 12³² corresponds to both, whilst 12³⁵⁻⁶ corresponds to 3¹⁹. The matter of vv. 14–16 suggests the closing stage of the ministry (cf. note on 2¹⁹—§ 18). In its traditional early position, as a prediction of the Passion, it is inconsistent with the Synoptics, especially as to the manner of the death of Jesus.[3] Note the following parallels with what goes before this section and also with the section which follows:

8²⁸	When you shall have lifted up the Son of man.
12³⁴	You say, The Son of man must be lifted up.
3¹⁴	So must the Son of man be lifted up.
12³⁵⁻⁶	Walk while you have the light, lest darkness overtake you . . . believe in the light.
3¹⁹	Light is come into the world, and men loved the darkness rather than the light.
12⁴⁶	I have come as a light into the world that [men] may not remain in darkness.
3¹⁵, ¹⁶	Every one that believes . . . every one that believes.
12⁴⁶	Every one that believes.
3¹⁷	God sent not the Son . . . to judge the world, but that the world . . . might be saved.
12⁴⁷	I came not to judge the world, but to save the world.
3¹⁸	He that believes not has been judged already.
12⁴⁸	He that rejects me . . . has that which judges him.

[1] ET, XLIV.229.   [2] cf. L. Johnson in ET, L.934.   [3] BJ, 114.

This section, or part of it (vv. 16–21), is looked on by most modern writers as the leading example of evangelistic commentary. But our rearrangement entirely obviates the difficulty caused by the break at the end of v. 13. Here 3[14-21] is included in a public address of Jesus in Jerusalem.[4] Bernard[5] says: 'The title "Son of man" is never used in the Gospels in narrative, or in evangelistic comment, being found only in the report of words of Jesus himself.' It is His very last appeal to the nation, and in it, for the first and only time, He refers to Himself as 'the only-begotten Son'. This may be John's warrant for the use of the word '*monogenēs*' in his first Epistle (4[9]) and in his prologue to the Gospel. Mark (12[6]) quotes 'He had yet one, a beloved son' as spoken by Jesus at Jerusalem during the Last Week. Luke (20[13]) records 'I will send my son, my beloved'; but Matthew omits the word 'beloved', although he relates the rest of the Parable of the Wicked Husbandmen. That this phrase occurs in Jesus' last public address, probably in the Temple, agrees with John's custom of working up to a climax. 'The only-begotten One, himself of the nature of God' (1[18]) is the culmination of the prologue; 'God gave his only-begotten Son' (3[16]) is the crowning declaration of the public ministry; and 'My Lord and my God' (20[28]) is the high point of the Gospel.

SECTION 27

12[44-50].—See preceding section for parallels, and note the order of the parallel statements. This correspondence with the matter before and after 3[14-21] in its new position seems to indicate that this is its original place. Westcott[1] notes that this paragraph has no connexion with its traditional context.

[4] cf. *BJ*, 114.   [5] *BJ*, 112.   [1] *WJ*, Intro. II.6.1.

SECTION 28

12⁵⁰   . . . what things I speak—even as the Father has said to me, so I speak.

---

³⁶ᵇ   These things did Jesus speak, and went away and hid from them . . .

12³⁶ᵇ⁻⁴³.—Many accept the transposition of 12⁴⁴⁻⁵⁰ and 12³⁶ᵇ⁻⁴³; the latter apparently being the evangelist's reflection on the now completed public ministry of Jesus, so that it naturally follows it.

The above rearrangements (§§ 17–26 in particular), of course, greatly increase the bulk of ch. 12, but not unduly. Reckoning the amount of matter given by each evangelist from the arrival at Bethany to the beginning of the Last Supper, John, including ch. 12 and the eight strayed sections, has 106 per cent as against Mark's 100, Luke's 79, and Matthew's 187.

SECTION 29

13¹⁻³⁵.—The thirteenth chapter begins the second and concluding portion of the Gospel proper. Many modern arrangements introduce chh. 15 and 16 after 13³⁰ or ³¹ᵃ, whilst others bring them in after v. 32. In all these cases 'my commands' (15¹⁰) are referred to without anything to show what they were.

13³¹⁻² seems to be the conclusion of what precedes,[1] and expresses the thought of Jesus that now (13²⁶⁻³⁰) He has fired the train that leads to the consummation of His

[1] cf. *SFG*, 271.

F

death.[2] But after this outburst of relief He turns to the preparation of the Eleven for the events of the immediate future.[3] He begins with a note of unwonted tenderness: 'Little children (*teknia*)', which diminutive does not recur in the Gospels. [Even 'children (*tekna*)' is recorded only once (Mark 10[24]) of Jesus when addressing the disciples, although 'paidia' (often='little children') occurs at John 21[5], where it='lads'.][4] Jesus then announces his impending departure. This is suitable to the beginning of the discourse. Again, in v. 34 we find the words, 'new command', and the word 'new' is not used when the command is twice repeated at 15[12] and [17]—which suggests that 13[34] is the first occasion of its mention.

SECTION 30

13[31]   So when [Judas] had gone out, Jesus says, Now is the Son of man glorified . . .

[33]   Little children . . . where I am going you cannot

[34]   come. . . . A new command I give you, that you love one another; even as I have loved you that

[35]   you love one another. By this will all men know that you are my disciples, if you have love one to another.

15[9]   Even as the Father has loved me, I also have loved you . . .

[12]   This is my command, that you love one another even as I have loved you.

[13]   Greater love has no one than this, that one lay down his life . . .

[2] cf. Brooke in *PCB*.   [3] cf. *SFG*, 277.   [4] *M & M*, *Voc.*, *s.v.*

15⁹⁻¹⁷.—This section appears to be the continuation of 13³¹⁻⁵. The command of 13³⁴, to 'love one another', is twice repeated, as is the avowal of Christ's love to His disciples. That He loves (*agapān*) His disciples and that they are to love one another is mentioned only in these two sections of the Last Discourses. In a review of Wendt,[1] who puts chh. 15 and 16 after 13³⁵, G. W. Stewart,[2] while not adopting the transposition, says: 'It is true that there does seem to be a certain connexion of thought between 13³⁴⁻⁵ and ch. 15, in which we find a further reference to the commandment to love one another (vv. 12–17).' The statement, 'I chose you . . . that you may go and bear fruit' (15¹⁶), would seem rightly to precede the statements, 'He that abides in me . . . he it is that will bear much fruit', and 'In this is my Father glorified, that you bear much fruit' (15⁵, ⁸).

SECTION 31

15⁹	. . . Abide in this love of mine.
¹⁰	If you keep my commands you will abide in my
¹⁷	love . . . These things I command you, that you love one another.

14¹⁵	If you love me you will keep these commands of mine . . .
²¹	He that has my commands and keeps them, he it is that loves me . . .
²³	If any one love me he will keep my word . . .

14¹⁵⁻²⁴.—The combination of the disciples' loving Christ, or, abiding in His love, and the keeping of His commands,

¹ *The Gospel according to St John*—Eng. Trans. by E. Lummis.
² *Exp*, VI.vii.146.

or, words, is found only here and in the last preceding section—15[10], 14[15, 21, 23, 24], and is introduced by the last sentence of 15[9]. The word 'command', either as noun or verb, is used by Jesus to His disciples only in §§ 28, 29, and 30.

In the declaration, 'I will request the Father, and he will give you another advocate' (14[16]), the word 'another' —which does not recur in this connexion—would seem to indicate the first mention of the 'advocate'.[1] P. V. Smith[2] suggests that 14[15-24] should follow 15[10]; and also says: '14[16-17] would appear naturally to have preceded the other [references to the Spirit] . . . [while that] in ch. 16 must have followed one or more of the others.' Hence this section seems to be suitably placed as in our rearrangement. Mears[3] also has the sequence—15[1-10], 14[15-24].

SECTION 32

15[1-8].—Having spoken thus fully of the mutual love which is for ever to unite the disciples to their Lord and to one another, Jesus institutes (although John does not say so since all the Church was well aware of it)[1] the 'sign and seal' of that love—the bread and the wine. Mark tells us that at this point Jesus said, 'I tell you truly, I shall no more drink of the fruit of the vine till the day when I shall drink it new in the kingdom of God' (Mark 14[25]). From this He goes on to speak of Himself as 'the real Vine' and of His disciples as the branches or shoots which are to 'bear much fruit'. Bernard[2] suggests that the Eucharist was followed by 15[1ff.]

[1] ET, LVII.219-20. [2] The Fourth Gospel, 143-4. [3] The Gospel of John.
[1] See FGH, 20. [2] BJ, 478.

SECTION 33

15²   Every branch in me which bears fruit he cleanses
that it may bear more fruit . . .

8   In this is my Father glorified, that you bear
much fruit, and so shall you become my disciples.

---

18   If the world hates you, (you) know that it has

19   first hated me. . . . I chose you out of the world,

20   therefore the world hates you. . . . If they per-
secuted me they will persecute you also.

15¹⁸–16²³ᵃ.—Bernard suggests that 'he cleanses it' may
be anticipatory of 'they will persecute you'. The union
of the disciples with Christ will be recognized not only
by the Father but by the world: hence they will be treated
by it as their Master was treated (cf. 13³⁵ and 17¹⁴; also
1 John 3¹ᵇ and ¹³).

SECTION 34

16¹⁹   Jesus said, Are you inquiring . . . about . . .

20   A little while and you will not behold me? Truly,
truly I tell you, You will weep and lament . . . but
your sorrow will be turned into joy. . . .

22   I will see you again and your heart will rejoice,

23   and your joy no one takes away from you. And in
that day you will not inquire of me about anything.

14¹   Let not your heart be troubled: believe in God and
believe in me . . .

4   Where I am going you know, and the way you
know.

⁵   Thomas says to him, Lord, we do not know
where you are going: how do we know the way?

14¹⁻¹⁴.—Jesus continues His exhortation to confidence
previously begun (16²²⁻³ᵃ) with: 'Let not your heart be
troubled.' Thomas's question could not well come before
16⁵. Bernard[1] says that 14⁵ must come later than 16⁶.
Some ancient authorities prefix 'And he said to his disciples' to v. 1—apparently thought necessary by some
scribe feeling a sense of abruptness arising from the dislocation of the text. A few omit v. 14, not having the
key (16²³ᵇ) to the solution of its peculiarity (see notes on
next section).

SECTION 35

14¹³	And whatever you ask in my name, this will I do, that the Father may be glorified in the Son.
¹⁴	If you ask anything in my name, I will do it.
16²³ᵇ	Truly, truly, I tell you, Whatever you ask the
²⁴	Father, he will give you in my name. Ask, and you shall receive, that your joy may be complete . . .
²⁶	In that day you will ask in my name . . .

16²³ᵇ⁻³³.—The 'Truly, truly, I tell you' of v. 23b would
seem to require an immediately preceding statement about
'asking' (see note on § 16). Hence it cannot well follow
v. 23a (§ 32), 'in that day you will not inquire of me . . .',
which appears to look back to v. 19: 'Jesus knew that
they wished to inquire of him. . . .' Commentators usually

[1] *BJ*, 503.

stress the distinction between 'ask' and 'inquire'.[1] Bernard, however, suggests that the emphasis in v. 23a is on the pronoun: 'You will not inquire of *me*.' But in its new context the passage vv. 23b–24 interprets 14[13-14], where alone the words 'I will do it' occur (twice). In v. 23b this is shown to mean: 'The Father . . . will give it you *in my name*.' The teaching of this Gospel is that what the Father does, the Son does, as stated at 5[19], and applied at 10[28-9]: 'No one shall snatch them out of my hand . . . no one can snatch them out of the Father's hand'; also 15[26], 'the Advocate . . . whom I will send', and 16[7], 'I will send him to you'; taken along with 14[16], 'the Father . . . will send you another advocate', and 14[26], 'Whom the Father will send *in my name*'. Similarly in 14[18], 'I will not leave you friendless: I am coming to you', there is a difficulty in deciding whether Jesus Himself is meant or whether the words refer to v. 16, 'He will give you another advocate . . . the Spirit'. This apparent confusion has led some to suppose that the Spirit and the Son are identical (cf. the ambiguity of 'the Lord the Spirit' in 2 Corinthians 3[17]). But again, what one member of the Trinity does, all do (5[19 ff.], 14[23], 10[38], etc.). As J. S. Banks[2] says: '. . . all Divine action is that of the whole Godhead.'

The statement, 'I came out from the Father and have come into the world; again I leave the world and go to the Father', and the disciples' reply, 'Now you are speaking plainly . . .' (16[28-9]), would seem necessarily to come later than the question of Thomas: 'We know not where you are going; how know we the way?' (cf. § 33).

[1] See Trench, *New Testament Synonyms,* § xi; cf. *ANT*, 365.
[2] *The Chief Corner Stone* (ed. Davison), 177.

SECTION 36

16³³　　These things have I spoken to you that in me
　　　you may have peace. In the world you will have
　　　anguish, but, Courage! I have overcome the world.

14²⁵　　These things have I spoken to you while abiding
　　　with you . . .

27　　Peace I leave to you; my peace I give to you
　　　not as the world gives give I to you. Let not your
　　　heart be troubled . . .

14²⁵⁻³¹.—The conclusion of the discourses, as indicated by
the latter part of v. 31: 'Arise, let us go from here.'
V. Burch[1] and others have this sequence. Until after the
resurrection the word 'peace' is found only at 16³³ and
14²⁷. R. H. Strachan[2] notes the parallels, 16³³—14²⁷
(peace), 16³²—14²⁸ (Father), 16³¹—14²⁹ (believe), 16³³—
14³⁰ (world). See also note on next section.

SECTION 37

13³⁶⁻⁸.—In the traditional order this section has nothing
to connect it with its immediate context, although it
would fit in after 13³³, if that were the end of a section,
which, however, is not the case. It is sometimes suggested
that Peter's question must of necessity have come before
the statements of 16²⁸⁻⁹, but there is no obvious place
for it. It must, however, come after 16⁵.[1] P. V. Smith[2]

[1] SMJ.　　[2] SFG, 272.
[1] BJ, 503; also F. J. Brown in ET, LVII.220.　　[2] The Fourth Gospel, 27.

thinks that 16³¹ should precede 13³⁸. The editor may have put it after 13³⁵ in order to get it as near as possible to 13³³. It might be expected that Jesus would make some definite mention of His death on this occasion, but though He refers several times in these discourses to His 'going to the Father', John does not record His saying anything of the manner of His departure (cf. Mark 8³¹, etc.). But 14²⁵⁻³¹ evidently means 'farewell', admitting of no further doubt that the Master is leaving His disciples. The breaking-point, however, is reached only with the last words: 'Arise, let us go from here.' This naturally involves forsaking the safety of the Upper Room and going out into the streets of the city at night, which Jesus had carefully avoided doing up to this time (Mark 11¹¹, ¹⁹), and Peter is alarmed at the consequences likely to follow, and in fear cries out: 'Lord, where are you going?' (cf. 11⁸, ¹⁶).[3]

SECTION 38

17¹–18¹³.—In the traditional order Jesus and the disciples appear to leave the Upper Room after 14³¹, and chh. 15 and 16 seem to record sayings spoken on the way to Gethsemane, which, however, they do not reach till 18¹. This makes it impossible to guess the place where the prayer of ch. 17 was uttered. But in our rearrangement the whole of chh. 13 to 17 belongs to the Upper Room. The long discourse ends with the command of 14³¹, when all stand up, and Jesus prays aloud in the presence of the eleven. P. V. Smith[1] says: 'The command to the disciples to stand with a view to departure is

[3] See *MJ*, 284–6 for other suggestions.   [1] *The Fourth Gospel*, 28.

naturally followed by our Lord's prayer. . . .' Then 'when Jesus had said these things he went forth with his disciples across the ravine of the Kedron . . .' (18¹).

SECTION 39

18¹²   So the band of soldiers and the officer in command and the Jewish guards seized Jesus and
13   bound him, and they led him first of all to Annas.

19   So the High Priest questioned Jesus about his disciples and about his teaching.

18¹⁹⁻²⁴.—It is sometimes suggested that Caiaphas rather than Annas would conduct the inquiry of vv. 19–23, and so v. 24 is brought forward to follow v. 13 or v. 14, while the cursive 225 and Cyril of Alexandria place it between v. 13a and 13b. Accepting the hint given by these last, we put vv. 19–24 after v. 13a. None of the Synoptics mentions Annas in this connexion, and Matthew 26⁵⁷ says: 'They that had seized hold on Jesus led him away to Caiaphas the High Priest.' Mark and Luke mention only 'the High Priest', without naming him. It would seem likely, since the office was hereditary according to the Law, that strictly religious Jews would still regard Annas as the real High Priest even after his deposition by the Roman power. Matthew and Mark never name Annas, but Luke, on the only occasions when he mentions Caiaphas by name (Luke 3², Acts 4⁶), puts Annas before him; and if Blass's conjecture on Acts 5¹⁷, adopted by Moffatt in his *New Translation*, is correct, then Annas is the only High Priest mentioned by name at that place. A. Plummer[1] notes that at 11⁴⁹ Caiaphas is spoken of as

[1] *Camb. Gk. Test.*

'one of them', and apparently is not presiding over the Council. Bernard says: 'The council was an informal one, and Caiaphas was not presiding.' If, however, he did not preside on that occasion, it is quite possible that he did not do so at the equally informal examination of Jesus (18[19-23]), but that Annas conducted the proceedings on both occasions. Headlam[2] says: 'That the first examination was before Annas . . . may well be an instance of inside knowledge.'

We include the transposition of §§ 38 and 39 with considerable hesitation; for, not only does Mark (15[53-72]) separate Peter's entry into the courtyard of the High Priest from his denials by his account of the first inquiry, parallel to John's traditional order; but also, as Bernard points out, John's custom is to use the name 'Simon Peter' at his first mention in any incident, and 'Peter' alone in continuation of the incident. This rule, however, does not appear to be invariable, e.g. 13[9] (but in that place there is some slight MS. authority against it) and 20[6]; also in the appendix (21[7]), where 'Simon Peter' follows 'Peter' in the same incident, with only three words intervening.

Although in this rearrangement Peter's entry into the courtyard is narrated not only after Annas' inquiry, but also after Jesus' dispatch to Caiaphas, yet the denials would seem to have more or less coincided with at least the former event. John's account of the first denial is much more precise than that of the Synoptists and appears eminently likely. 18[5] says: 'that disciple . . . entered with Jesus into the courtyard of the High Priest.' Absorbed as he was in what was happening and about to happen to his Master, he was not watching his companion's movements, but vaguely supposed that Peter would follow him into the courtyard; then, finding he had not done so, he went to the door to look for him. It would seem that

[2] *FGH*, 21.

Peter had been refused admission, since 'that disciple . . . spoke to the portress and brought in Peter'. This girl knew 'that disciple' as a follower of Jesus, so challenges Peter: 'Surely, you are not one of this man's disciples, are you?' From this we infer that the first denial may have occurred even before the beginning of Annas' interrogation.

It may be that Mark drew up his narrative in the order he does with a view to the fact that even while Jesus was 'witnessing the good confession' in the High Priest's chamber above, Peter in the court below was denying Him; and that the editor of John followed Mark in this matter when arranging the dislocated sheets of the original draft. But it is also possible to suppose that the evangelist himself wrote in the traditional order for the same reason as we have supposed Mark to do, and at 18²⁵ followed his usual custom of beginning afresh with 'Simon Peter' when reintroducing that apostle into the narrative. But if v. 25 followed v. 18 in the original draft the writer would not repeat the statement that 'Peter was standing and warming himself', which in that case must be due to an editor.

SECTION 40

18²⁴   So Annas dispatched him,
bound as he was, to Caiaphas the High Priest;

---

¹³ᵇ   for he was father-in-law to Caiaphas, who was
       High Priest that year.
¹⁵   Now Simon Peter followed Jesus, and another
       disciple . . .

18¹³ᵇ⁻¹⁸.—Verse 13b would appear to follow v. 24 better than it follows 13a, since Caiaphas has not there been mentioned, and v. 14 may be a gloss. Howard[1] notes that in 18[14], where is repeated from 11[50] Caiaphas' counsel that it were 'better that one man should die' rather than the whole people, there is the *accusative and infinitive* construction; 'better for one man to die', instead of John's usual idiom of *hina with subjunctive*—perhaps here is the mark of a redactor.

In the traditional order Peter's 'warming himself' occurs in two different localities, unless the statement of v. 24 —'Annas sent (*apesteilen*) him to Caiaphas' (who on this interpretation was present)—means 'handed him over to Caiaphas' in order that he might go on with the trial in the place where they already were. Some have supposed that both High Priests lived in the one 'High Priest's house', although in different apartments; in which case Jesus was taken from one room to another, perhaps crossing the courtyard. At any rate Peter's denials all occurred in the High Priest's courtyard. It is generally thought that the usual place of meeting of the Sanhedrin was somewhere within or near the Temple.[2] But all four Gospels distinctly show that Jesus was taken to the house of the High Priest, whether Annas or Caiaphas, and the Temple is not mentioned. *The Jewish Encyclopedia*, in the article 'Jesus of Nazareth', says that according to the Talmud, Hanan's bazaars were on the Mount of Olives, and probably, therefore, his house, which would thus become the appropriate place for the trial by the Sanhedrin; which, indeed, just about that time removed its place of session there.[3] So that on this occasion, at least, the Council met at Annas' house. This would be all the more likely if Mark's statement is strictly correct that the gathering under Caiaphas was not really a trial but only a 'consultation' as to the charge to be brought before

[1] *FGRC*, App. B.   [2] *HDB*, IV.399.
[3] See also Schürer, *History of the Jewish People*, etc., Div. II, § 1, 190–3.

Pilate (Mark 15[1]). Jesus was to be got rid of—the only question was how it was most surely to be done. If then it was not intended to be a legal trial, the place of meeting was almost certainly not the Temple. Bernard[4] says: 'Nothing is told here of the proceedings, which were only formal, as the decision had been already reached at the irregular meeting in the house of Annas.'

SECTION 41

18[18]   . . . and they were warming themselves; and Peter also was standing with them and warming himself.

25b   So they said to him, Surely you are not one of his disciples, are you?

18[25] to end.—The word 'they' in v. 15 cannot refer to any persons mentioned in the six preceding verses as found in the traditional order, but must refer to v. 18, and so most suitably follows it. For further remarks on vv. 25–7 see notes on §§ 39–40. It is possible that 25a is original, and that 18b is the interpolation.

In common with the part of the Gospel before 18[25], the part which follows that point as far as 20[31] has been subjected to many different theories of redaction and of various sources, but there seems no possibility of any dislocations of the text having taken place, such as we have been considering: the narrative moves on in what appears to be the necessary chronological order throughout. If any of the sheets of this portion were disarranged at any time, there could be only one way of rearranging them—into the order of the original draft. 20[30-1] is plainly the conclusion toward which the evangelist has all the time been working.

[4] *BJ*, 605.

The story of ch. 21 should have been told before the
'conclusion' of 20³¹. Obviously it was an afterthought,
added perhaps to balance the account of Peter's denials
and to correct the rumour concerning 'the beloved disciple'.[1] When the work was about to be published v. 24,
or part of it, was added by authority, and v. 25 may have
been appended by some one who knew a number of
non-canonical narratives concerning Jesus.

THEORY OF THE DISLOCATIONS

The following list, numbered 1 to 41 in the first column,
shows in the second column the sections of the Gospel
in the order of the present arrangement. The third column
gives the supposed number of pages which contained the
section as originally written; the fourth the number of
lines which any one page of the section occupies as printed
in Westcott and Hort's *New Testament in Greek* (smaller
edition); and the fifth states how the section ends—'I'
indicating that the incident is completed, and that a fresh
incident begins with the next section; 'p' that a paragraph
is completed; 's' a sentence; and 'phr.' a phrase (this last
occurring only at the end of No. 20).

No.	Section	Pages	Lines	Ending
1	1¹–2¹³ᵃ	14	8·2	s
2	5¹⁻⁴⁷	10	8·6	p
3	7¹⁵⁻²⁴	2	9·1	I
4	3²²⁻³⁰	2	8·6	I
5	4¹⁻⁵⁴	12	8·5	I
6	6¹–7¹⁴	18	8·7	p
7	7²⁵⁻⁹	1	9·4	p

[1] See *INT*, 264.

No.	Section	Pages	Lines	Ending
8	7^{40-3}	1	6·4	p
9	7^{30-2}	1	6·9	s
10	7^{44-52}	2	6·8	I
11	7^{37-9}	1	6·8	I
12	9^{1-41}	9	8·7	p
13	8^{12-20}	2	9·2	p
14	10^{19-29}	2	9·4	p
15	10^{1-18}	4	8·8	s
16	$10^{30}-12^{19}$	18	9·1	s
17	$7^{53}-8^{11}$	2	8·5	p
18	2^{13b-25}	3	8·5	p
19	8^{31-59}	7	8·4	I
20	3^{1-13}	3	8·6	phr.
21	3^{31-6}	1	9·5	I
22	12^{20-33}	3	8·8	p
23	7^{33-6}	1	8·3	p
24	8^{21-30}	3	6·7	p
25	12^{34-6a}	1	8·2	s
26	3^{14-21}	2	7·8	p
27	12^{44-50}	2	6·7	I
28	12^{36b-43}	2	7·0	I
29	13^{1-35}	8	8·2	s
30	15^{9-17}	2	8·1	p
31	14^{15-24}	3	6·6	p
32	15^{1-8}	2	7·5	p
33	$15^{18}-16^{23a}$	7	8·8	p
34	14^{1-14}	3	8·5	p
35	16^{23b-33}	3	6·9	p
36	14^{25-31}	2	6·8	I
37	13^{36-8}	1	6·7	I
38	$17^{1}-18^{13a}$	9	8·4	s
39	18^{19-24}	2	5·9	p
40	18^{13b-18}	2	5·9	s
41	18^{25} to end			

Obviously, in the six longer sections it would be possible to divide by a different figure for the number of pages and so obtain a different result as to the number of lines. Thus, No. 12 may be reckoned to have either 9 pages, each of 8·7 lines; or 10 pages, each of 7·8 lines. But in more than half the sections the quotient is not open to doubt. Other possible sections are:

Section 1—2^{1-13a} =3 pages, each of 7·9 lines
Section 16—10^{1-10a} =2 pages, each of 9·0 lines
                10^{10b-18} =2 pages, each of 8·8 lines
Section 29—13^{31b-35} =1 page of 8·5 lines
Section 31—16^{16-23a} =2 pages, each of 8·8 lines

F. W. Brown[1] suggests that 2$^{1-11}$ may follow 4^{45}.

G. H. C. Macgregor[2] says: 'Even in the most carefully written MS. there would be greater difference between the contents of the pages than in a printed book.'

In Codex Sinaiticus (א), now in the British Museum, at the opening which shows the ending of Luke and the beginning of John (published in facsimile), there are seven complete columns (and an incomplete column containing the ending of Luke). Transposed into terms of WH text, these seven columns respectively occupy 14·4, 14·9, 14·9, 13·8, 16·0, 16·8, 15·9 lines: an average of 15·2 lines with a range of 3 lines—practically 20 per cent on the average figure.

Taking this variation of *Cod. Sin.* as a convenient standard—10 per cent either way—and allowing for a normal page of 8·6 lines, the present arrangement shows fourteen sections not greater than the maximum and twelve not less than the minimum, with one (No. 32) ambiguous (see below). Section 3 (7$^{15-24}$) has sometimes been taken as the standard of length, but our list shows

[1] *ET*, LVII.317.   [2] *ET*, XXXIII.76.

that it exceeds the average by almost the full allowance.

Of the seven complete columns of *Cod. Sin.* mentioned above, three end in the midst of a word, which is completed in the next column, while the remaining four end with a word, which in one case completes a sentence; but none ends a paragraph or an incident. But of our sections, eleven (not counting the ending of the Gospel) end with the completion of an incident; seventeen with a paragraph; eleven with a sentence; and one with a phrase. This seems to indicate quite clearly that the disarrangement of the Gospel cannot be due to the accidental displacement of the leaves of a properly written fair copy, but that there must have been a first draft, written at least partly on odd sheets which were afterwards deranged. F. J. Paul[3] says: 'In some cases at least the writing was first inscribed, by the author or his amanuensis, on loose leaves, and only when the writing was complete were these loose leaves gummed together. . . .' P. V. Smith[4] suggests that the contents of this Gospel were written on separate sheets at different times. F. J. Brown[5] says: 'The disorder . . . may . . . have occurred in the rough notes of the amanuensis.' J. M. Thompson[6] thinks that the manuscript dislocated must have been in codex form [i.e. not a 'roll'].

Now in a rough draft the writer would not have such regard to the appearance of the finished page that he would break off in the midst of a word, but would finish the word and probably the sentence before beginning on another page or sheet. If, say, a line or two were added to an otherwise normally full page (i.e. the last page of the section), or letters were written closer or smaller—this last being fairly common in *Cod. Sin.*—in order to complete the sentence or paragraph, the average content

[3] *HJ*, VII.4.   [4] *The Fourth Gospel*, 34. Also *FGG*, 382.
[5] *ET*, LVII.217.   [6] *Exp*, VIII.ix.425.

would not be greatly raised if there were several pages to the section; but if there were only one or two pages the quantity of matter would be decidedly above the average. This corresponds to the figures for the sections Nos. 7 and 14 (each of one page), which attain the maximum; and Nos. 3, 13, and 16 (each of two pages), which approach it. No. 21 exceeds the maximum by 1 per cent. The omission (with B) of 'the Spirit' would more than cancel this excess.

There is also the possibility that notes would be added in the margin with a view to their incorporation into the text of the fair copy. This may be the real explanation of the length of some of the sections just mentioned. The fact that in general the virtual uniformity in the length of our supposed pages affords little evidence of marginal addition, may indicate what is probable in itself, namely that the author knew exactly what he wished to say, having told these stories so often that their form had become fixed. There are a few places where a sentence seems to be displaced, perhaps because it was first written in the margin, and included in the fair copy at the wrong point, e.g. at 10^{12-13} we read: 'The hired man . . . sees the wolf coming, and leaves the sheep and runs away (and the wolf seizes the sheep and scatters them); for he is only a hired man, who cares nothing for the sheep.' The words in brackets might be better placed as a separate statement after the ending of the main statement. Perhaps 11^5 is such an instance: Moffatt brings it in between vv. 2 and 3. On the other hand, the editor or some early copyist may have made additions of his own, e.g. the parentheses of 1^{21}, 2^9, 4^8, 6^{23}, 11^2, $18^{9,\ 14,\ 32}$, 19^{39}, 21^{14}, and perhaps 12^{33}. None of these adds anything fresh: they are deductions from the context, immediate or more remote. 3^{24} presumes a knowledge of the Synoptic tradition, and may belong to the autotype, but may equally well come from a later hand. Bernard suggests that 4^{1-2} was 're-written'. 4^{10} is omitted by אD and some Old Latin copies.

There are, in addition to those mentioned above, another thirteen sections which occupy a definitely smaller number of lines. Now a writer might begin a fresh incident on a fresh page or sheet, even though some space was left on the page last written on, especially when taking up the work anew after an interval. Bernard[7] suggests such a blank space after 12^{36a-43}. This would be most likely if loose sheets were being employed, and would account for six of the short sections. No. 10 ends the story of the guards being sent to arrest Jesus and coming back without Him; Nos. 11 and 37 each contain a complete incident on a single page; No. 27 records the ending of our Lord's public ministry; No. 28 the evangelist's reflection on the result of that ministry; and No. 36 the conclusion of the discourses in the Upper Room.

It would seem likely that the author wrote his work, perhaps at odd times, partly if not altogether on single sheets of papyrus.[8] Sir F. Kenyon[9] says: 'The shorter Epistles, such as the second and third of St John, or St Paul's letter to Philemon, would have been written on a single sheet of papyrus, like the ordinary private letters of which many examples have been found.' In all probability these sheets would mostly be of about the same size. We note, however, that there are six groups of pages with especially small content included in sections 8-11, 24, 27-8, 31, 35-7 and 39-40. As shown above, six of these sections—Nos. 10, 11, 27, 28, 36, and 37, each completes an incident, and this may account for their brevity; but of the others, Nos. 8, 24, 31, 35, and 39 each completes only a paragraph, and Nos. 9 and 40 only a

[7] *BJ*, xxx.   [8] See P. V. Smith, *The Fourth Gospel*, 34.
[9] *The Story of the Bible*, 30.

sentence. The real reason for the small content of at least some of these sections may be that the sheets on which they were written were of smaller size than the rest, possibly larger sheets cut in two. In such a case it would be natural to use several such smaller sheets consecutively, as is agreeable to their places in our arrangement, where, except No. 24, they are found in groups of four or more pages. No. 32 appears to have one page of smaller size (like the three pages of No. 31—these together making a group of four) and one of larger size, comparable to the pages of section 33 which follows it. This may have occurred also in No. 26. If, for these smaller pages we assume an average content 6·6 lines of WH text, allowing as before ten per cent of variation either way—all fall within these limits except §§ 39 and 40, which are over seven per cent smaller than any others. This may be held to confirm our hesitation as to their transposition.

It is possible that papyrus was employed of which the *recto* had already been used for other matter. If not throughout, this may have happened in some parts of the original draft. It would account for the eight sections which consist each of only a single page, as well as for the others which have an odd number of pages. It may also account for the strangeness of 4^{1-2}, where, a single sheet having overlapped the rest of the pack, the top edge may have been damaged so that some words were illegible. The same applies to 6^{23}, that verse beginning the sixth page of the section. If this is the case it is probable that in both instances the relevant matter was found on only one side of the sheet, since no confusion is apparent at the places corresponding to the top lines of the other side.

In section 1, when the extra stanzas are taken out (they occupy 14·8 lines of WH text), the rest of the section consists of 12 pages, each of 8·3 lines. Now if the first few sheets, if no more, of this section had its matter on only one side of the sheet, then the additional stanzas, written on both sides of an extra sheet, would be slipped into the pile between sheets 1 and 2. Verses 1-8 occupy one page, and vv. 9-14 a rather full page. When writing out his fair copy, the editor, having finished page 1—one side only—would continue with the extra sheet, and when he had completed all he found on the face of it (vv. 9-14, *ex hypothesi*), did not turn it over to write out what was on the reverse side (vv. 16-18), since he supposed that this sheet like No. 1 had its matter on only one side, but went on with sheet 2 of the original (v. 15), and had written it before finding that the extra sheet had further matter on the other side. This he then added before continuing with vv. 19ff. His alternative was to spoil his new roll or codex by a large erasure or a marginal addition almost at its beginning. That the person writing out the Gospel in fair copy for the first time makes this error near the beginning of his work is natural enough, as he has not 'got into the swing of it'. This suggests that he may not have been a professional writer.

Some inference may be drawn as to the actual size of the sheets used. The *Rylands Gk.* 457 papyrus appears to have been part of a *de luxe* copy of the Fourth Gospel. The page was some $8\frac{1}{4}$ by 8 inches in size, and contained 18 lines, each having about 31 letters. The writer of a first draft would be likely to use a much smaller and cheaper size, and would write more closely. The *Egerton 2* papyri (New Gospel Fragments), unfortunately, are imperfect, retaining only part of the margin at the top and one side. But the restoration of the lines gives an approximate width of $5\frac{1}{4}$ inches, each line containing 24-5 letters, although the length of the page cannot be determined.

For our first draft we suggest a sheet of $4\frac{1}{2}$ inches wide by $5\frac{1}{2}$ inches in length, each page containing 16 lines of about 23 letters. This allows a margin rather less than *Eg. P. 2*, and somewhat closer writing. Fifteen lines to the page would nearly approach our assumed minimum, and seventeen lines the maximum as based on *Cod. Sin.* The *Codex Alexandrinus* (A) varies between 49, 50, and 51 lines to the column.[10] If used papyrus was employed, the writing may have run parallel to the longer sides, and the addition or omission of one line would produce a possible variation somewhat in excess of that assumed above.

It may be thought that so many sections have been made[11]—some of them rather small—that it would be possible to put several of them in any one of a number of places, so that the presumed new order is too precarious to build upon. But this is not the case: §§ 1–3 are shown to be connected together in order, as also §§ 4–5, 6–21, 22–8, 29–31, 32–7, and 38–41. The connexions are of course not so clear in some cases as in others, and some may be found unacceptable; but it would appear that none of the series of connected sections can change places with any other series.

THE TRADITIONAL ORDER

A complete theory of the dislocations would seem to require some suggestion as to how our presumed original order was changed into the traditional order, which, except perhaps for the place given to the Cleansing of the Temple, appeared on the whole to be fairly satisfactory.

[10] See article 'Manuscripts' in *DCG*.

[11] Moffatt's *Trans. N.T.* has 20 sections, with a number of odd verses in addition; *MJ* has at least 33.

The following table compares the suggested new order with the traditional order, the sections being numbered as in our rearrangement. In addition these sections are collected into eight (quite arbitrary) divisions, as shown, the purpose of which will appear later.

Div.	A. New Order	B. Traditional Order	C. 'Strays'	D. Totals of B+C
I	(1) 1^1–2^{13a}	(1) 1^1–2^{13a}		
			(18) 2^{13b}–25	
			(20) 3^1–13	
			(26) 3^{14}–21	1^1–3^{21}
II	(2) 5^1–47	(4) 3^{22}–30	(21) 3^{31}–6	
	(3) 7^{15}–24	(5) 4^1–54		
	(4) 3^{22}–30 $\Big\} =$	(2) 5^1–47		
	(5) 4^1–54	(6) 6^1–7^{14}		
	(6) 6^1–7^{14}	(3) 7^{15}–24		
	(3^{22}–7^{24}, less 3^{31}–6)			3^{22}–7^{24}
III	(7) 7^{25}–9	(7) 7^{25}–9	(23) 7^{33}–6	
	(8) 7^{40}–3	(9) 7^{30}–2		
	(9) 7^{30}–2 $\Big\} =$	(11) 7^{37}–9		
	(10) 7^{44}–52	(8) 7^{40}–3		
	(11) 7^{37}–9	(10) 7^{44}–52		
	(7^{25}–52, less 33–6)			7^{25}–52
			(17) 7^{53}–8^{11}	7^{53}–8^{11}
IV	(12) 9^1–41	(13) 8^{12}–20	(24) 8^{21}–30	
	(13) 8^{12}–20	(12) 9^1–41	(19) 8^{31}–59	
	(14) 10^{19}–29 $\Big\} =$	(15) 10^1–18		
	(15) 10^1–18	(14) 10^{19}–29		
	(16) 10^{30}–12^{19}	(16) 10^{30}–12^{19}		
	(8^{12}–12^{19}, less 8^{21}–59)			8^{12}–12^{19}
V	(17) 7^{53}–8^{11}			
	(18) 2^{13b}–25			
	(19) 8^{31}–59			
	(20) 3^1–13			
	(21) 3^{31}–6			
	(22) 12^{20}–33	(22) 12^{20}–33		
	(23) 7^{33}–6			
	(24) 8^{21}–30			12^{20}–36a
	(25) 12^{34}–$6a$	(25) 12^{34}–$6a$		
	(26) 3^{14}–21			
VI	(27) 12^{44}–50	(28) 12^{36b}–43		
	(28) 12^{36b}–43 $\Big\} =$	(27) 12^{44}–50		
	(29) 13^1–35	(29) 13^1–35		
	(12^{36b}–13^{35})			12^{36b}–13^{35}

Div.	A. New Order	B. Traditional Order	C. 'Strays'	D. Totals of B+C
VII	(30) 15^{9-17}	(37) 13^{36-8}		
	(31) 14^{15-24}	(34) 14^{1-14}		
	(32) 15^{1-8}	(31) 14^{15-24}		
	(33) $15^{18}-16^{23a}$	(36) 14^{25-31}		
	(34) 14^{1-14}	(32) 15^{1-8}		
	(35) 16^{23b-33}	(30) 15^{9-17}		
	(36) 14^{25-31}	(33) $15^{18}-16^{23a}$		
	(37) 13^{36-8}	(35) 16^{23b-33}		
	$(13^{36}-16^{33})$			$13^{36}-16^{33}$
VIII	(38) 17^1-18^{13a}	(38) 17^1-18^{13a}		
	(39) 18^{19-24}	(40) 18^{13b-18}		
	(40) 18^{13b-18}	(39) 18^{19-24}		
	(17^1-18^{24})			17^1-18^{24}
	(41) 18^{25} to end			

Anyone dealing with loose sheets of written or printed matter must often have found that when reading such sheets one after another he has reversed the order of the sheets by putting them down, in the order of reading them, *face upwards* in a pile, so that, say, six sheets ABCDEF are found in the new order FEDCBA. Now suppose these six sheets contain §§ 14 and 15 of this Gospel ($10^{19-29, 1-18}$), then when the editor finds them in this new order he rearranges FEDC into CDEF (10^{1-18})—no doubt finding the needful clues in the pages themselves—and also rearranges BA into AB (10^{19-29}), but leaves these two sets of sheets in the order in which he finds them, so making the traditional order of 10^{1-29}. We note that $10^{30}-12^{19}$ follows at once; so that in 10^1-12^{19} there is only one displacement, but three sections have to be reckoned because of the break.

This kind of accidental displacement, along with the consequent editorial rearrangement, probably accounts for many of the remaining transpositions. Reference to the above table shows that a similar reversal of sections has occurred in some places. In the following list each of these is indicated by an asterisk (*) in the margin.

In 1^1–2^{13a} there is no major displacement.

2^{13b}–3^{21} has strayed from ch. 12.

* In 3^{22}–7^{24} the sections 5^{1-47} and 3^{22}–4^{54} (less 3^{31-6}, astray from ch. 12) exchange places, but are still followed by 6^1–7^{14}, while 7^{15-24}, which it is generally agreed originally followed ch. 5, has been put at the end of this group.

[N.B.—When the original order is restored it is seen that ch. 5 comes immediately after 2^{13a}.]

* In 7^{25-52} the sections 7^{40-3} and 7^{30-2} are reversed, but have 7^{37-9} placed between them, while 7^{44-52} follows on, and 7^{33-6} has strayed from ch. 12.

7^{53}–8^{11} is also from ch. 12.

* In 8^{12}–12^{19} the sections 9^{1-41} and 8^{12-20} are reversed, while 8^{21-59} has strayed from ch. 12.

* [10^1–12^{19} is mentioned above.]

Between 12^{19} and 12^{36b} all the eight strayed sections have been omitted [see below on division V], but 12^{20-36a} remains.

* In 12^{36b}–13^{35} the sections 12^{44-50} and 12^{36b-43} exchange places and 13^{1-35} follows on.

13^{36-8} is placed before instead of after the next following group.

In 14^1–16^{33} the sections 14^{15-24}, 15^{1-8}, 15^{18}–16^{23a}, 16^{23b-33} (together forming quite two-thirds of the whole) are still in their original relative order; but each of the first two pairs is separated by one section (of two pages) belonging to other parts of these Last Discourses; while the last pair are brought together, 14^{1-14} being omitted from between them.

* In 17^1–21^{25} only 18^{19-24} and 18^{13b-18} exchange places, the rest being in correct sequence.

This accounts for the whole of the Gospel except division V, of which eight out of the ten sections are in complete disorder. In view of the general orderliness of the rest of the Gospel it seems right to assume that the loose sheets on which these sections were written (three of them comprise only one page; three, two pages; three, three pages; and only one has more than three pages) were accidentally scattered, and were later inserted where they were supposed to fit.

We observe further that in the traditional order the sections numbered 4 and 5 are separated by No. 21 (one page), as are Nos. 13 and 12 by Nos. 24 and 19. Nos. 7, 16, 29, and 28 are in their supposed original places, while Nos. 6, 9, 10, 12, 13, 14, 15, 16, 27, 28, 30, 38, and 40 are only one place removed, and Nos. 2, 4, 5, 8, 11, 32, and 35 are removed two places; leaving (apart from division V) only 3, 33, 34, and 36 out of position by three; No. 30 by five, and No. 37 by seven places. On Nos. 22 and 25 see below.

We note further that Nos. 2–6 form one block (division II), with No. 21 intruding between Nos. 4 and 5, which otherwise would be in correct sequence. Nos. 7–11 form another such block (division III), with No. 23 intervening between Nos. 9 and 11. Nos. 12–16 form a similar block (division IV), with Nos. 24 and 19 coming between Nos. 13 and 12. Nos. 27–9 (division VI) form a small block with Nos. 22 and 25 immediately preceding. Nos. 30–7 are all in their own block (division VII), as are Nos. 38–40.

We also note that the above blocks, as blocks, along with sections 1 and 41, are in the same sequence both in the traditional order and in our rearrangement. In the process of editing, Nos. 1 and 41 could not be placed in any but the right order—at the beginning and end respectively of the Gospel. Of the blocks, the statement of 3²³, that 'John was baptizing at Ænon', marks out division II as belonging to the earlier part of the narrative; and No. 4 may lead its division because of that statement. The block of Nos. 7–11 appears to refer to the feast of Booths

(§ 11), which would suggest that it should follow division II which mentions that feast (§ 6). Division IV mentions two festivals, which settle its place. Division VI is in its only possible position; and Nos. 22 and 25 are rightly put between the two divisions last-mentioned. Division VII necessarily follows No. 29 and precedes No. 38. All the same, although suggestions are offered as to why these divisions have been arranged as they are, yet it is just as likely that the editor found them for the most part in this order and made only minor adjustments.

We note that in our rearrangement division VII follows the sequence frequently suggested by modern writers— chh. 15, 16, 13 (end), 14—except that 15¹⁻⁸ and 15⁹⁻¹⁷ exchange places, as also 16²³ᵇ⁻³³ and 14¹⁻¹⁴; but 14¹⁵⁻²⁴ is brought into the discourse before the Institution of the Eucharist, and 13³⁶⁻⁸ comes at the end of this division instead of at its beginning.

Only the eight strayed sections remain—Nos. 17, 18, 19, 20, 21, 23, 24, and 26. Obviously, with Nos. 22 and 25 they form one block, which must somehow have become separated from the rest of the Gospel. This, together with the fact already noted, that every other section is found in its own division, would seem on the one hand to negative the suggestion that some editor purposely altered the order of events, and on the other hand would appear definitely to support the theory of accidental dislocation; the sections of division V being afterwards inserted by the editor or some other person in the places which they occupy in the traditional text.

Nos. 22 and 25 (12²⁰⁻³⁶ᵃ) would be seen to belong to the Last Week on account of 12²³ and 12³⁴ respectively. Perhaps also the 'Greeks' of 12²⁰ were thought of as belonging to 'the world' of 12¹⁹.

No. 18 (2¹³ᵇ⁻²⁵) is dated 'at the Passover' (2²³), and is located in Jerusalem; and since 4⁴⁵ mentions that Jesus had attended a festival there, and no other account of a visit to that city remained unplaced (see above on 'blocks'), especially as 2^{13a} mentions a Passover and is apparently intended to begin a narrative of events in the metropolis, while 2^{13a} and ^{13b} form a perfect connexion, the editor would feel obliged to insert it in front of division II, although he was quite aware that Mark had put a similar account into his story of the Passion Week.

No. 20 (3^{1-13}) might appear to the editor to illustrate No. 18 (2^{23-5}), so he placed it immediately after it.

No. 26 (3^{14-21}) would be put after No. 20 because of the words 'the Son of man' in 3^{13} and 3^{14}. This may have debarred No. 21 (3^{31-6}) from its rightful place, and it may have been inserted after No. 4 because of a supposed correspondence between 3^{30} and 3^{31}: 'He must increase . . . He . . . is above all.'

No. 17 (7^{53}–8^{11}) could not be put after 12^{19} when once $12^{20ff.}$ had been attached to the latter; but it seems to have some correspondence with No. 13 (cf. 8^{11} and 8^{15}).[1]

As for Nos. 23 (7^{33-6}) and 24 (8^{21-30})—the fact that 'the high priests and the Pharisees dispatched guards to arrest him' (7^{32}) may have suggested to the editor that Jesus thereupon saw the beginning of the end, so said: 'Yet a little while am I with you, and then I go to him that sent me' (7^{33}). The similar words of 8^{21}, '*Again* . . . he said, I am going away . . .', must come later than 7^{33}, but follow an occasion when the authorities are known to have wished to arrest Jesus (8^{20}).

No. 19 (8^{31-59}) may follow 8^{30} because of the words 'believed him' in vv. 30 and 31; whilst 8^{59} tells of Jesus leaving the Temple, where He had been teaching (8^{20}).

That these ten sections of division V were originally together is supported by the fact that they can thus be arranged in one block and that, except for 12^{20-36a}, they

[1] cf. *TRJ*, 150; also P. V. Smith, op. cit., 20.

are found in the traditional text in just two blocks, each of four sections, namely 2^{13b}–3^{36} (less $3^{22\text{-}30}$) and 7^{33}–8^{59} (less $7^{37\text{-}52}$ and $8^{12\text{-}20}$). It is true they are not in their supposed original sequence within these blocks, but that may only be a sign of the accidental dislocation by which they became separated from the rest of the Gospel. It would, however, appear to mean that the editor found them more or less together, although obviously out of place where they were—perhaps at the beginning or end of the Gospel.

These sections contain less than one-eighth part of the Gospel. Yet it is some of these eight strayed sections which were first observed to be ill-fitting and have raised most of the questions relating to the composition and historicity of this Gospel.

It is not to be supposed that only division V was disturbed, but probably much of the rest of the Gospel. The narrative portions, however, could be put in order for the most part by comparison of one page with another, e.g. the eight long sections (also 18^{25}–20^{31}) consist mainly of narrative. But the teaching would not so easily reveal its natural sequence, e.g. that of the Last Supper, where the seven small sections (only one has more than three pages) are in considerable disorder.

That the outline of the Gospel taken generally, in blocks, as above, is seen to be the same both as traditionally received and as (supposedly) originally composed, accounts for its order of contents having seemed so satisfactory up to quite recent times, and leads to the inference that the author left his work in correct chronological sequence. It would further appear that the editor was careful to retain as far as possible the order of the manuscript as it came to him, rearranging only when it seemed necessary to do so,[2] and that he never divided the papyrus sheets which

[2] cf. *FGRC*, 132–3, 141.

came to him, but sought only to place them in orderly sequence. That he was unable to put the whole into its original order after its disarrangement is due to those habits of the author which have already been noticed—in some cases writing a few words or lines on an otherwise full page in order to complete a sentence or paragraph; and in other cases leaving part of a page blank after completing a paragraph or incident, rather than filling up the page with a few words belonging to another incident or paragraph. In this way the natural clue of an unfinished sentence or narrative was eliminated, and the editor was left without guidance as to the sequence of the sections. No doubt in many instances he did find points of connexion and was able to restore many sheets to their proper places. It is, of course, likely that the draft had been disarranged and rearranged more than once. W. F. Howard[3] says: 'It was manifestly left by the author in a state which made a certain disarrangement of the papyri possible, if not inevitable. . . .'

The above theory of the editor's arrangement of the sections into the traditional order would seem to imply that neither the author nor anyone who had been connected with the writing of the Gospel could have taken part in preparing it for publication. This would appear to indicate that some time—perhaps some few years—had elapsed between its composition and its being made known to the Church, and it may also imply a change of locality. It could have been written, say, during the exile in Patmos (Revelation 1[9]) if such occurred, and been brought to Ephesus on the author's return after the death of Domitian (A.D. 96); and may possibly have been found among his effects after he himself had passed away. L. Jackson[4] says: '[The evangelist] never published it; when first it emerged from its depository he had, in all

[3] *XJ*, 18.   [4] *The Problem of the Fourth Gospel*, 122.

likelihood, gone to his rest. . . .' In any case, as V. H.
Stanton[5] says: 'The writing of the Gospel would be a
work performed in private, of which few could have direct
knowledge.' The whole of the dislocations may have
occurred after the manuscript was discovered, perhaps
under the circumstances suggested below. Streeter[6] says:
'It is possible that the Gospel was published posthumously.
If so, the author may have died leaving a pile of tablets
or a number of loose dictated pieces on sheets of papyrus,
and a pupil may have arranged them as best he could
for publication.'

RELATION TO THE SYNOPTIC GOSPELS

In the traditional order John offers an outline of the
ministry of Jesus different from that given by the other
three Gospels. The difference is modified in the present
rearrangement. The following table compares our rearranged order of John with the order of Mark and Luke—
Matthew being omitted, partly as following Mark, and
partly as arranging his material on other than a chronological basis.

Ministry of Jesus	Mark	Luke	John
A Preparatory	1^{2-13}	3^1-4^{13}	$1^{6-8,\ 15,\ 19-34}$
B Before the Ministry in Galilee			$1^{35}-2^{13a}$, 5^{1-47}, 7^{16-24}, 3^{22-30}, 4^{1-42}
C Galilean Ministry	$1^{14}-7^{23}$	$4^{14}-9^{17}$	4^{43-54}, 6^{1-17}
D Northern Itinerary	$7^{24}-9^{50}$	9^{18-50}	7^1

[5] *GHD*, iii.280.   [6] *FGG*, 382.

Ministry of Jesus	Mark	Luke	John
E Southern Itinerary	10^1	9^{51}	7^2–11^{54}
		(?) 17^{10}	(except as noted)
F Last Journey and Last Week	$10^{2\text{ff.}}$	(?) $17^{11\text{ff.}}$	7^{53}–8^{11}, 2^{13b-25} 8^{31-59}, 3^{1-13}, $31-6$, 7^{33-6}, 8^{21-30}, 3^{14-21}, $11^{55\text{ff.}}$

A.—The Synoptists appear to record the work of the Baptist before the Baptism of Jesus, whilst John's account in 1^{19-36} gives the Baptist's testimony after the Temptation, 1^{15} being indeterminate. Edersheim puts the Baptism and Temptation of Jesus before 1^{19}.

B.—It is sometimes urged that, since at 1^{37-51} some disciples have gathered about Jesus, John is giving another version of the call recorded in Mark $1^{16\text{ff.}}$ But the former gives, not a call to discipleship, but the story of the first acquaintance of Jesus with men who before were strangers to Him.[1] G. Milligan[2] calls it 'a personal relationship'. The latter call is to immediate discipleship based on previous acquaintance and on His public preaching.[3] In a review by H. Hogarth[4] Père Lagrange is said to hold that some disciples had met Jesus before the occasion mentioned in Mark 1. A. E. Garvie suggests that Galilean disciples may have been sought only when no response came from Jerusalem and Judaea; and says:[5] '. . . the small company of disciples whose attachment to Jesus is recorded in John 1^{35-51} followed Him only for a time; and had to be recalled when the Galilean ministry began.' It is commonly supposed that Peter was the first of all the disciples to recognize Jesus as the Christ, but it is possible

---

[1] cf. *G-S*, 7. [2] *DCG*, I.52. [3] cf. *CHE*, 403.
[4] *LQHR*, July 1938, 362. [5] *GBD*.

that John, and perhaps his brother James, had known it (in some measure) long before—it may be from 2¹¹—and that because of this Jesus could take them with Him to Jerusalem and in their hearing make His great statements of 5¹⁶⁻⁴⁰. Possibly Judas Iscariot was the only fruit of the Judaean ministry.

Again, it is often suggested that, since the Synoptists (following Mark) indicate that Jesus did not begin His Galilean work until after the imprisonment of John, the records of the Fourth Gospel should be rejected. But John does not say that there was any public ministry in Galilee at that time, but on the contrary definitely states (2¹²): 'they remained there not many days.'⁶

That the Synoptists omit the early Judaean ministry would seem to be due to the reliance of Matthew and Luke on Mark,⁷ and to Mark's reliance on the testimony of Peter,⁸ who, after his introduction to Jesus (John 1⁴²), does not appear in His company again until after the work in Capernaum had already begun (cf. Luke 5²⁻³, Mark 1¹⁶).⁹ Mark has no information about the early days, but John has definite knowledge, and so includes it in his narrative. Peter, however, supports John's account by speaking (Acts 1²¹⁻³) of 'those who accompanied us . . . beginning with the baptism of John'. W. F. Howard¹⁰ says: 'Mark's leap from the Temptation to the Galilean mission leaves ample room between for the arrest and imprisonment of John.' J. A. Findlay¹¹ writes of 'the considerable period which must have elapsed between His Baptism and the opening of His campaign in Galilee . . .', and goes on to say: 'It is to be noted . . . that the first outburst of murderous bitterness in Galilee is coincident with the visit of *scribes from Jerusalem.*' C. J. Cadoux¹² says: 'The Fourth Evangelist . . . seems to have known

⁶ *BJP*, 87–8.   ⁷ *HE*, ii.15, etc.   ⁸ cf. *GHT*, 37–8.   ⁹ *GBD*, 69.
¹⁰ *AC*, 121.   ¹¹ *What did Jesus teach?*, 112–13.   ¹² *CLJ*, 53–6.

a good deal about this interval, and he determined to use it.'

C.—From our rearrangement it appears that John mentions the first sign (4^{46-54}) and the last (6^{5-13}) of the Galilean ministry, thus intimating that he knew the whole of it. E. Hoskyns[13] says: 'The Evangelist is not ignorant of a longer ministry in Galilee. . . .' H. Scott Holland[14] says: 'He has no occasion to use [the Galilean ministry], but he lets us know that it is there.' John deliberately omits all the intermediate events, since, on the one hand, they did not directly bear on his special purpose (20^{31}), and on the other hand, they had already been given to the Church by Mark—not that everything had been said, but that Mark had given a fair typical view. This indicates that John knew the Second Gospel and that he approved it—otherwise he would have contradicted it.[15] In fact, there are several instances of his apparent correction of some of its details. But he not only knew it, but expected his readers to know it, too. If then John knew enough to judge the historicity of Mark,[16] he must have known the whole story. This suggests that he was an eye-witness, or at least the careful recorder of the testimony of an eye-witness. And as the healing of the Officer's Son is not mentioned in Mark, John probably knew the Third Gospel also (see notes on § 5). Of course there is the alternative that John himself had so fully narrated in the Church the incidents of the Galilean ministry that he knew that all the members were aware of them. But in his Gospel he is dealing with the deeper themes of the Incarnation.

D.—Here again, having mentioned the fact, John omits the details, which had been made known through Mark. In the Synoptics the public ministry in Galilee ends soon after the Feeding of the Five Thousand (unless Mark 8^{1-10}

---

[13] *The Fourth Gospel*, 202.   [14] *HFG*, 169.   [15] *FGH*, 8.   [16] *HE*, iii.39.

is brought in). Many of Jesus' disciples have forsaken Him (6^{66}); He has deliberately broken with the Pharisees[17] (Mark 7^{1-23}); and on the other hand the preaching of the Twelve seems to have stirred up the civil authority, and Jesus saw the wisdom of retirement. F. C. Burkitt[18] suggests that the [later] secret passage through Galilee was a precaution against premature arrest by Antipas. So the Feeding may have been intended as a Farewell; and the work in Southern Galilee ended with Jesus' open repudiation of Jewish tradition. Burkitt also[19] notes 'the long absence from Galilee indicated in Mark $7^{24, 31}$', and the 'small amount of tradition connected with this period [8 months (*GHT*, 93)] which very likely took up more than half the time included in the ministry . . .'; yet, strangely enough, denies (op. cit. viii) that there is room in Mark for the Raising of Lazarus. But as the Feeding took place in the springtime, twelve months before the Crucifixion, it would appear that a sufficient period is left both for Mark's account of the Northern Itinerary and for John's account of the visits to Jerusalem and elsewhere.

E.—That the visits to Jerusalem are not directly mentioned in Mark may be due to the circumstance that Peter accompanied his Master there only on the last occasion. Except at 6^{68} he is not mentioned in John between 1^{42} and 13^6. As the events of chh. 5, 7, 9, and 11 took place in or near the city we presume Peter was not present, as also at 2^{1-11}.[20] After all, Peter had a wife and family to support, and they did not travel about with Jesus. Neither Peter's temperament, his upbringing, nor his Galilean accent (Mark 14^{70}, Acts 2^7) fitted him for life in the metropolis until Pentecost changed him. Indeed it is likely

---

[17] F. W. Lewis, *Disarrangements, etc.*, 12–13.

[18] *ERE*, VI.339, art. 'Gospels'; also *GHT*, xiv.

[19] *GHT*, xii.   [20] *BJ*, clxxxiii; also *FGH*, 24.

that most of the Galilean disciples were left behind or sent out on some mission when Jesus went to Jerusalem (cf. Luke 10[1]), except at the Last Passover.[21]

But that Jesus had exercised His ministry in the Holy City before the Last Week is supported by many hints in the Synoptics. R. H. Lightfoot[22] notes that 'I was daily with you in the Temple' (Mark 14[49]) is not sufficiently accounted for by the few days of the Passion Week. A. E. Brooke[23] says: 'The improbability that a teacher like Jesus of Nazareth should so completely neglect the capital of His country till it was too late to do anything but suffer death, must be one of the most obvious inadequacies of the Synoptic account . . . the Johannine account is altogether more probable.' A. E. Garvie[24] asks: 'Is it not . . . certain that Jesus as the Messiah of the Jewish nation could not be content to offer Himself for its acceptance or rejection in the comparatively insignificant province of Galilee, but must have felt constrained to press His claims upon it at the very centre of its national life at the seasons when Jews from all parts of the world had come together to worship?' A. S. Peake[25] writes: 'It is intrinsically unlikely that Jesus, conscious of His messianic vocation, should be content to work simply in the provinces and make no appeal to the religious capital of Judaism, and the centre of its constituted authority, till the last week of His life.' H. V. Stanton[26] says: 'The enmity of the [rulers] in Jerusalem must have been prepared for. The work of Jesus in the country districts could hardly . . . inspire their determination to destroy Him. The two or three days of teaching in Jerusalem . . . would have been altogether insufficient to bring their hostility to a head. . . .' W. Temple[27] asks: 'How was it possible for

---

[21] cf. H. R. Reynolds in *HDB*, II.710b; also *BJP*, 85.

[22] *History and Interpretation in the Gospels.*   [23] *CBE*, 297.

[24] *GBD*, 70.   [25] *Intro. N.T.*, 214.   [26] *HDB*, II.244a.   [27] *TRJ*, Intro.

the Lord to plan the preparations for the Triumphal
Entry and the Last Supper if He had never been in
Jerusalem . . .?'[28] After the close of the Northern
Itinerary, Mark 10[1] says that Jesus went to Judaea and
Peraea.[29] This cannot well refer to the final journey,
since if He had gone through Judaea He would not
afterwards go through Peraea to get to Jerusalem.
The statement may be intended to indicate that there
was a ministry in Judaea (also in Peraea, as mentioned
in John 10[40-2]),[30] but that Peter did not attempt
to narrate its details, as he had not been present.
H. B. Swete[31] remarks that in contrast to Mark 1–9,
Mark 10 has no further note of time or place.

If for purposes of inquiry we suppose Luke's special
source (L) to constitute his first collection of incidents
in the ministry of Jesus, and that it may be read *seriatim*,
then that part of it which is included in Luke 9[15]–18[14]
appears to correspond in some measure with Mark 10[1]
and with John's account of the visits to Jerusalem, Judaea,
and Peraea. C. J. Cadoux[32] has a detailed scheme largely
similar to this and the following paragraphs, but includes
Q matter also.

In 9[51] Jesus starts off for the Metropolis, probably to
attend the feast of Booths. As he had not recently been
there He may have wished to be sure how far He could
venture before committing Himself and His disciples, so
took with Him, say, only James and John (Luke 9[52-4]),[33]
who apparently were familiar with the city (18[15, 16], 19[27]).[34]

The lawyer of Luke 10[25ff.] may be the same person as
'one of the scribes' (Mark 12[28]), and the incident may
have happened at Jerusalem—the scene of the parable of
the Good Samaritan is on the road 'from Jerusalem to

[28] cf. *FGH*, 9.   [29] cf. *GHT*, 96–7.   [30] *FGH*, 7–8.
[31] *Gospel according to St. Mark.*   [32] *CLJ*, Ch. 6.
[33] cf. *GHT*, 96–7; also *FGH*, 41.   [34] cf. C. A. Briggs in *ET*, XV.68–9

Jericho'; and the next verse tells us that 'Martha welcomed him into her house'.[35]

The matter from 'L' in Luke 11–12 is small in extent, and appears to have nothing suggesting time or place. Luke 11[9-52] and 12[1b-12, 22-59] together form much the largest insertion from 'Q' found in the Third Gospel after 9[50]. Hence we continue with ch. 13 as perhaps originally following ch. 10 in 'L'. In 13[2-5] Jesus matches the Galileans murdered by Pilate [in the Temple at Jerusalem] with those [Jerusalemites] 'on whom the Tower of Siloam fell'. This is followed immediately by the parable of the Barren Fig-tree (13[6-9]; cf. Mark 11[12ff.]).

John does not say where Jesus was between Booths and Dedication, but in Luke 13[22] we find Him again 'journeying toward Jerusalem', apparently from either Galilee or Peraea—'Get away, Herod wants to kill you' (13[31]). Luke 14–16 belongs almost exclusively to 'L', but does not seem to suggest any particular time or place.

After the raising of Lazarus John says Jesus retired to Ephraim. When the time came for the Last Journey He may have gone to Galilee to collect His disciples, since in Luke 17[11] we find Him 'on the way to Jerusalem . . . passing through the midst [perhaps=borders] of Samaria and Galilee'. Possibly the word *sustrephomenōn* (Matthew 17[22])[36] refers to this occasion. 'Matthew' may have thought that here Jesus was beginning His last journey through Galilee to go to Jerusalem, so says: 'As they were gathering themselves together, Jesus said, The Son of man is about to be delivered up. . . .' Mark 9[30-1] says: 'Coming out from there they proceeded through Galilee . . . he . . . said, The Son of man is delivered up. . . .' A. C. Headlam[37] suggests that as some, if not all, of the

[35] cf. C. A. Briggs in *ET*, XV.68–9.

[36] Read by אB, etc., and RV margin; cf. F. W. Green on *St Matthew* (Clarendon Bible), *in loc.*

[37] *Jesus Christ in History and Faith.*

apostles were in the way going up to Jerusalem to the
last Passover—not in the company of Jesus, but expect-
ing to meet Him there—'Jesus was there, going on in
front of them; and they were filled with amazement . . .'
(Mark 10[32]). A. C. Deane[38] writes to the same effect.[39]
T. R. Glover[40] offers a different explanation.

We do not suggest that these possible coincidences of
Luke with John are necessarily to be taken in the above
order, or even that Jesus took just that number of jour-
neys to Jerusalem. Luke may not have had sufficient
information on these points, but may simply have been
told of certain incidents as occurring while Jesus was on
His way to and visiting the city. We do suggest, however, that Luke's account leaves room for John's narrative,
and at least so far supports it.

Then in Luke's story of the Last Week several notes
are found which are not easily explicable on the supposition of only a few days' teaching in the metropolis,
e.g. 'He was daily teaching in the Temple' (19[47]); 'On one
of the days, as he was teaching in the Temple' (20[1]); 'Every
day he was teaching in the Temple, and every night he
went out . . .' (21[37]—cf. John 18[2]); and 'The feast of
Unleavened Bread drew near' (22[1]). These statements
seem to suggest that altogether Jesus spent some considerable time at Jerusalem,[41] although Luke did not
know the precise details, any more than he knew the
details of the days succeeding the Resurrection (24[44-53]),
the account of which he revises when writing his second
treatise (Acts 1[1-10]).

F.—The four Gospels differ in their accounts of the
Last Scenes—Mark being largely quoted by Matthew and
less fully by Luke.

[38] *Jesus Christ*, 100.   [39] *GHT*, 96-7.
[40] *Jesus of History*, 173-4.
[41] cf. A. E. Garvie in *Abingdon Bible Commentary*, 1061 b.

On the whole question of the relationship of John to the Synoptists we find that he omits everything they have said, except what he needs for the statement of his own scheme. Instead of explaining why he omits, we have rather to explain why he inserts any particular matter already mentioned by the others. H. Scott Holland[42] says: 'Whenever he wishes to use for his own purposes incidents and scenes which appear in the common tradition, he leaves the tradition out of account and works over the ground on his own account with entire freshness and originality. . . . For some reason he stands above the common tradition and not below it.' A. E. Garvie[43] is 'convinced that the parallels [between John and the Synoptics] are not close enough to prove, and that the differences are great enough to disprove, literary dependence'. C. E. Raven[44] says: 'whatever the value of his work, it was at least drawn from an original source.' B. H. Streeter[45] writes: 'He was a personage who possessed, and was recognized as possessing, a claim to write with independent authority.'

J. Gardner-Smith seeks to show that John was unacquainted with the Synoptics. But that John in 'many passages . . . differs from the Synoptics for no apparent reason'[46] may be due not to ignorance of them, but to his personal knowledge of the facts. Our rearrangement seems to show that he knew the whole story. Whilst, however, he may well have known both Mark and Luke, yet it would appear to be unnecessary to suppose him to be in literary dependence on them: he sets forth his story quite independently. 'Form-criticism' has reminded us that the Gospel history must have been well known to all the churches by means of oral tuition;[47] and John could assume his readers' knowledge of the principal events

[42] *HFG*, 118.   [43] *GBD*, 38.   [44] *JGL*, 207.
[45] *FGG*, 426.   [46] *G-S*, 92.   [47] *G-S*, 93.

I

of the ministry of Jesus—not only such as are mentioned
in the Second and Third Gospels, but, since he himself
had been engaged in oral teaching in Asia for a number
of years, in the Fourth Gospel also; indeed, there would
be many other traditions, some of them written (cf. Luke
1[1-4]), which were not included in any of the Gospels; and
John may have corrected some of these in his work. W. F.
Howard[48] writes: 'We can confidently affirm that by this
time the basic material of the Gospel was part of the
common heritage of the Church.'

It seems quite impossible that a fairly full Gospel
tradition should not have been known in Ephesus, where
Paul had spent three of his most active years; and it
would seem that Mark's work, written some thirty years
before, probably Luke's also, must have been known there
in the decade A.D. 90–100. The reason that John, in spite
of its great dissimilarity to the others, could be accepted
by the Ephesian Church, was that its author was known,
and that his teaching was familiar to the members there.
As Sir F. Kenyon[49] says: 'The express attribution of its
authorship, in the final chapter, to the Beloved Disciple,
must have been made at a time when there were many
persons living who could confirm or deny its accuracy.'
There is of course another side to the question. Burkitt[50]
says: 'That St Luke's Gospel was a private venture is
sufficiently indicated by the preface. That St Mark's
was so is sufficiently indicated by the narrow escape it
ran of being lost altogether.' These facts suggest that
these Gospels may not have been known to the writer of
the Fourth Gospel. Even this Gospel, as Th. Zahn[51] points
out, was 'directed not to the general public, but to a
definite circle of readers'.

But the total impression left by a careful perusal of

[48] *XJ*, 178.   [49] *The Bible and Modern Scholarship*, 50.
[50] *GHT*, 274–5.   [51] *The New Schaff-Hertzog*, vi.204.

John is that the author knew quite well at least the Second
Gospel, and this not, as is often suggested, because of the
matters he relates in common with Mark, but because of
the things he omits, e.g. in his narrative of the trial of
Jesus by the High Priest he would seem carefully to avoid
mentioning what has been said by Mark (14^{55-65}), not that
he did not know it, but that it was already known by
everybody through Mark's story. This is not the same
as supposing that everybody knew the general facts, which
were much wider than Mark's account: John stops just
where Mark begins. Again, whether or not we transpose
§§ 39 and 40, John says nothing at all of the proceedings
under Caiaphas beyond his statement that 'Annas dispatched him . . . to Caiaphas', and the further statement:
'So they lead Jesus from Caiaphas to the Praetorium';
not because he was ignorant of what happened, but because
Mark (15^1) had told that, 'In the morning the chief priests,
with the elders and scribes, and the whole council, held
a consultation . . .'. Similarly he mentions Mary Magdalene
alone of the women who went early to the tomb (20^{1-2}),
although he knew that others were also present; for he
relates that Mary said: '*We* know not where they have
laid him.' Many other instances might also be adduced.

It is frequently affirmed that the words, 'Get up, take
your mat and go home' (5^8), are taken from Mark's story
of the healing of the paralytic, especially as the word *kra-
battos* is used by both writers, and not by Matthew or
Luke. But this word is known to have been in common
use in Galilee where both Peter and John were brought
up, as 'Matthew' and Luke were not (cf. *otarion* (ear)
(Mark 14^{47}, John 18^{10})—not found elsewhere in the Greek
Bible).

It is sometimes further suggested that John, for some
purpose of his own, has transferred the scene of that cure
from Capernaum to Jerusalem. But our rearrangement

shows that the healing at Jerusalem took place before that at Capernaum. It may be that on the latter occasion Jesus made the healing a challenge to the 'Pharisees and teachers of the Law who had come out from . . . Jerusalem' (Luke 5¹⁷), possibly recognizing one or more of His former opponents. In any case, why must He find new words for a situation similar to an earlier one?

Again it is said that John makes Jesus claim Messiahship in His early ministry as against the Synoptists, who for the most part only mention it in the later stages. John's purpose is clearly stated at 20³¹ and fully accounts for the marked differences between this Gospel and the other three. His theme is 'Jesus Christ the Son of God'.⁵² He indicates that Jesus declared Himself as the Messiah in His early ministry (4²⁶) as does Luke (4²¹), and our arrangement shows that these two sayings were uttered about the same time and in this order. Thus Jesus offered Himself as the Christ in His early ministry, i.e. in Samaria and at Nazareth. But in the rest of the Galilean ministry, until about its close, He did not usually declare it. Just as Paul on leaving Athens decided on preaching of a certain type (1 Corinthians 2²), so Jesus on beginning His work in Eastern Galilee may have decided not to proclaim Himself as Messiah, since His hearers misunderstood the term. C. J. Cadoux⁵³ says: 'As Jesus understood Messiahship in so different a sense from the Jewish public in general, He made no open claim to it.' Perhaps His experience at Nazareth had much to do with this decision, which was confirmed by the frequent cries of those mentally deranged, as at Capernaum: 'I know who you are— the Holy One of God', when Jesus said: 'Be muzzled!' (Mark 1²⁴). See also Mark 1³⁴: 'He did not permit the

---

⁵² cf. A. E. Brooke in *CBE*, 306–7.

⁵³ *The Historic Mission of Jesus*, 103; also quoted by H. G. Wood in *HJ*, XL.393–5.

demons to speak; for they knew him'; and Mark 3[11, 12].
But at Jerusalem, the religious centre of the nation, He
must necessarily put forth His claim. Yet even there He
did not baldly say, 'I am Messiah', except possibly when
solemnly charged by the High Priest at the Trial. When
challenged, as at 8[25], 'Who are you?', 8[53], 'Who do you
make yourself out to be?', and 10[24], 'If you are the Christ,
tell us plainly'—He gave no direct answer, since any title
would only have misled them. V. Taylor[54] says: 'Jesus
held His Messianic claims in check. Messiahship was His
secret.' H. R. Mackintosh[55] writes of 'the all but insur-
mountable difficulty of proclaiming Himself as the Messiah
without stirring into flame passions of a kind which would
have rendered the people deaf to His unique message.'
C. E. Raven[56] writes: 'In the social and political circumstances in Galilee, and until His followers had learned
something of the new character that He gave to [Messiah-
ship], such proclamation would have been fatal.'

[54] *ET*, LIX.150.   [55] *The Person of Jesus Christ*, 17–18.   [56] JGL, 215.

CONCLUSION

If the present rearrangement of this Gospel is accepted, even in general outline, several important inferences would seem to follow. The ensuing paragraphs mention only a few points which appear to arise from our scheme.

Our rearrangement gives a time-scheme of a little over two years,[1] divided into four periods.

1.—From some two or three months before a Passover up to a time not very long after it, including a visit to Jerusalem and a (probably short) sojourn in Judaea, possibly followed by another visit to the Holy City at, say, Pentecost. This period would thus extend over some three to five months, ending about the time when the Baptist was arrested. The 'four months to harvest' (4^{35}) is probably not a note of the time of year, but merely a proverbial saying.

2.—The ministry in Galilee as detailed in the Synoptics, extending over some ten or eleven months up to a second Passover, which occurred shortly after the Baptist's death.

3.—A more private ministry in the northern parts of Galilee (and perhaps beyond), occupied by 'the training of the Twelve', and culminating in Peter's Confession and the Transfiguration, which took place shortly before the feast of Tabernacles in the second year. This period covers some six months.

4.—Several visits to Jerusalem and neighbourhood, ending with a third (the last) Passover. This lasted about another six months.

It is commonly supposed that the Synoptic account gives the impression that the ministry lasted for only about a year. But a careful reading leads to a different

[1] cf. *CLJ*, 42, 89.

estimate. Possibly Luke thought of it in that way, since he mentions 'the acceptable year of the Lord', in which case his date of 'the fifteenth year of the reign of Tiberius Caesar' may mean A.D. 28, yielding A.D. 29 as the year of the Crucifixion. But Mark, among other notes, speaks of 'the green grass' (6[39]), which agrees with John 6[4] as denoting the springtime. C. J. Cadoux[2] says: 'The Fourth Gospel is built on a chronological scheme of Jewish festivals.' Wm. Temple[3] says: 'The Johannine chronology is the only one we have. . . . The Synoptic narrative is unintelligible unless something like the Johannine story is accepted. . . . Mark did not even purport to provide a chronological scheme. . . . The evidence to be set against the very clear and full chronological scheme by St John is negligible.' Streeter[4] says: 'John is the first and the only one of the Evangelists who attempts a chronology . . . it is the only one we have.' Raven[5] says: 'The advantage of historicity is with the Fourth Gospel.'

On the other hand R. Dunkerley[6] suggests twelve 'major coherents' and twenty-four 'minor coherents', i.e. incidents in the Synoptics which fit their places in the narrative so completely and 'coalesce so naturally that there is a presumption that they belong to each other, and that the resultant picture is historically sound'. The fact that the outline of events is now seen to agree with that found in the Synoptics indicates that the historicity of this Fourth Gospel is to be estimated on the same basis as theirs. It is not that John was trying to 'harmonize' his account with theirs, but simply that he was following the actual order of events as he remembered them.

In the traditional order some of our Lord's discourses seem to merge into comments by the evangelist. But in

[2] *CLJ*, 41.   [3] *TRJ*, Intro.   [4] *FGG*, 424.
[5] *JGL*, 202.   [6] *ET*, LVIII.133-6, 161-4.

the instances usually cited our rearrangement includes these paragraphs in Jesus' own addresses. This also reacts on the rest of the discourses and suggests that John was not soliloquizing, but reporting throughout.[7] Of course he has numerous comments of his own, mostly brief, which are plainly such. C. J. Wright's presentation of the theory of allegory[8] is deliberately based on the traditional order of events. But a careful study of the Gospel as here rearranged leaves on the mind the impression that the author, so far from allegorizing,[9] is concerned above the average to express every detail as precisely as possible.[10] The Gospel is chronologically arranged, which is more than can be said of Matthew, and not definitely of Mark; while Luke, although desiring to write 'in order', fails through lack of personal knowledge of the circumstances. Moreover, John everywhere lays stress on reality. It is not to the point to say that he meant spiritual reality. Those whose opinions he opposed would have said they meant the same. But if he had not built on historical reality he could not have exposed the various heresies of his time. He could not refute, say, Docetism with the declaration that 'Jesus Christ has come in the flesh', if at the same time he used imaginary instead of actual events to support his statements.[11] A. E. Brooke[12] says that the author 'could hardly find worse weapons with which to combat the so-called Docetism of his time than facts invented for the purpose'. And Wm. Temple[13] says: 'It is vital to St John's purpose that the events which he records should be actual events.' Streeter supports this (*FGG* 29f.). Hoskyns and Davey[14] write: '[In this Gospel] the foundation

[7] cf. M. Black in *ET*, LIX.175.

[8] *Meaning and Message of the Fourth Gospel*; also in *Mission and Message of Jesus*.

[9] cf. A. E. J. Robinson, art. 'Gospels', *EBr*, XIV.538a.

[10] cf. *DJL*, 79.   [11] *SFG*, 29–30.   [12] *CBE*, 311.   [13] op. cit.

[14] *The Riddle of the New Testament*, 238.

of the Church is shown to be the actual Words, Actions, Death and Resurrection of Jesus who came in the flesh.'

That this Gospel is now seen to be historically correct in its general presentation of the ministry of Jesus[15] tends to show that the author must have been one of his actual followers.[16] This he claims for himself in 1[14]: 'We beheld his glory. . . .' L. V. Lester-Garland[17] says: 'The first impression provoked by an attentive reading of the [Fourth Gospel] is that the wealth of unstudied detail indicates that it is the work of an eye-witness.' Sir F. Kenyon writes:[18] 'We have in the Fourth Gospel the reminiscences by an eye-witness of facts and discourses, often of a more intimate and private character than the public utterances recorded by the Synoptics. . . .' Raven[19] says: 'He is a witness and testifies in order that men may believe . . . .'

In his First Epistle the writer addresses his readers as 'little children', and obviously is an old man.[20] If he had been, say, 16 years of age when he became a disciple in A.D. 26–7,[21] he would be 85–6 in A.D. 96. Compare this, as does Th. Zahn,[22] with Polycarp, who declared: 'Fourscore and six years have I served [Christ]. . . .' He may have been urged, as stated in the Muratorian Fragment, by those who had listened to his teaching, to put it in writing for the future use of the Church, and in the end may have done so.[23] Or, if he were banished to Patmos 'on account of the word of God' (Revelation 1[9]), it is most

[15] cf. *FGH*, 30.
[16] cf. W. Sanday, *Criticism of the Fourth Gospel*, 74–97; also D. S. Cairns, *Study Bible: John*, 2.
[17] *HJ*, XXXVI.268.
[18] *The Bible and Modern Scholarship*, 24–5.
[19] *JGL*, 198.
[20] cf. B. W. Bacon in *HJ*, VI.133–4; also *FGH*, 36–8.
[21] *BJP*, 5.
[22] *New Schaff-Hertzog*, art. 'John the Apostle'.
[23] cf. *HE*, iii.24.

likely, since he could not be sure that he would ever return
to Ephesus, that he would wish to record in writing the
message he had been giving orally for so many years.
Then on the death of Domitian he may have been able
to return to his former home, taking his draft of the
Gospel with him—perhaps hoping to make it more perfect if opportunity served. That this was the case is supported by the fact of the addendum of 21[1-23]. No one
before Irenaeus mentions Asia as John's residence, and
this is made the occasion to doubt whether he ever lived
there. But the *argumentum e silentio* can scarcely be admitted here, since we have a similar absence of information
respecting the last years of Peter and Paul, not to speak
of less prominent apostles. James Vernon Bartlet[24] writes
of 'John the son of Zebedee, whose presence at Ephesus for
a period of years cannot be explained away by any confusion with another John'. He also says:[25] 'Asia . . . this
province Lightfoot was surely right in regarding as the
centre of gravity in the Church for a century or so after
the death of St Paul.' A. E. Brooke[26] agrees that 'the
least unsatisfactory explanation of the evidence . . . is
. . . that the Apostle did spend some years of his later
life in Ephesus. . . .' Possibly 21[1-23] was added after his
return, but was never properly amalgamated with the rest
of the work. Even if John did not go to Patmos it seemed
certain that as he felt his life nearing its end he would
desire to leave behind him a permanent record of his
teaching so far as it was not already included in the
Synoptic narratives, especially in view of the welter of
speculation arising from contact with Gentile cults in
Ephesus.[27]   He may well have sought to influence those
outside the Church as well as those within it, as C. H.

[24] *DCG*, II.309.   [25] *AC*, 15.   [26] *DAC*, I.628a.
[27] cf. J. A. McClymont in *HDB*, III.526a; also his *St John* (Century
Bible), 24–6.

Dodd[28] says: 'He retold the Gospel story in terms which would enable them to understand its deeper meanings, and win their assent.   He succeeded in his aim.'

There is every likelihood that John had told these and many other stories again and again from the beginning of his preaching, their contents being enriched throughout the years as points came back to his recollection. Stanton[29] says: '. . . large portions of [the Gospel's] contents had been imparted to the Church before they were here put together.'   And A. C. Deane[30] writes: 'We have no need to suppose that St John waited until some sixty years after our Lord's ministry to set down his account of it. . . .'   But on composing a permanent record he would carefully select and revise the incidents so that they might convey the right message to the Church.   This must have taken weeks and perhaps months.   Burkitt[31] says: 'No doubt the Gospel took many years to write.' And Howard[32] writes: 'The Gospel was probably the slow growth of many years of preaching, teaching, meditation, and reflection.'   If in the end, owing to the infirmity or death of the author some other person had to undertake the editorial arrangement of a large number of sheets, some of which were in disorder, the result might well be such as we actually find.

The attestation of 21[24] must be contemporaneous with the publication of the Gospel, as no documentary authority is known to omit it, and it appears to be the endorsement of the Ephesian Church.[33]   In that case it would seem to show that the author had passed away before his work was published.[34]   This agrees with the suggestion of our

[28] *The Bible Today*, 69.
[29] *GHD*, iii.284.
[30] *How to Enjoy the Bible*, 86–91.   See also *FGG*, 24.
[31] *ERE*, VI.342n.
[32] *XJ*, 18.
[33] cf. J. B. Mayor in *HDB*, III.282b.
[34] cf. E. F. Scott, *Fourth Gospel*, 104.

foregoing paragraph that the work may not even have been written out in fair copy before his decease, but was left to be edited by another person. Howard[35] says: 'The Gospel and the Epistles were written or dictated by the same venerable leader of the Church in pro-consular Asia. The Gospel . . . was *published* after his death.' The words, 'who testifies (*present tense*) to these things', may mean, 'in this Gospel'; and 'who wrote (*past tense*) these things', may mean, 'before his departure'.

The Apocalypse is not by the author of this Gospel, although the writer belonged to his circle. Howard[36] says: 'Johannes Weiss made one significant remark. These writings all came from the same circle, in the same region of the Church, about the same time. They reckoned on being accepted and understood by the same constituency.' The Apocalypse cannot well be earlier than Domitian, but may belong to the close of his reign.[37] J. E. Carpenter[38] puts it about A.D. 95. E. F. Scott[39] suggests *c.* A.D. 96. If it were published after John's death, about the same time as the Gospel, it would obtain a standing as his work —the name 'John' occurs in it four times—and such a claim could not easily be disproved after his decease. If he had been in Patmos the mention of this in Revelation 1[9] was intended to implement the acceptance of that work; and if it was known or believed that he had been engaged in writing, this also would facilitate its reception by the Church. It may be that the more or less simultaneous publication of the two writings 'queered the pitch' for the Gospel; whilst the necessity for attestation after the death of the author would breed suspicion in certain minds. Howard[40] says: 'The Lucan [anti-Marcionite] Prologue . . . closes with the sentence, "Afterwards John the

---

[35] *XJ*, 18n.   [36] *XJ*, 15.   [37] cf. Irenaeus *ap*. Eusebius, *HE*, v.8.
[38] *The Johannine Writings*.   [39] *The Revelation*, 28–30.   [40] *XJ*, 15.

Apostle, one of the Twelve, wrote the Apocalypse in the Island of Patmos, and after that the Gospel".' The association of the Gospel and the Apocalypse may further account for the opposition of the '*Alogi*', as also for a certain hesitancy found in the references of some early Fathers of the Church to this Gospel and its author.

The difficulty of accepting the Gospel was created by the author himself, partly by his delay in writing it, but perhaps still more by his deliberate omission of nearly everything contained in the Gospels already acknowledged; his apparent substitution of their spiritual meaning for the Sacraments themselves; and his seeming transformation of the teaching regarding the Lord's return. People of that day were no doubt as conservative in matters of religion as people today—'The old is good enough!'[41] But that this Gospel was early recognized and used is shown, not only by early versions and its occasional use by early writers, especially some of the Gnostics—Origen says that Heracleon (*c.* A.D. 160)[42] wrote a commentary on it—but particularly by the *Rylands Gk.* 457 and *Egerton* 2 papyri recently brought to light.

It is commonly supposed that Mark and 'Q' are the primary authorities for the life of Jesus. The Second Gospel, however, is by one who was not an eye-witness of what he records, although he probably includes much that he derived from Peter; whilst the First and Third are certainly composite, and were written, at least in their present form, by men who may never have seen Jesus. But that the Fourth Gospel, taken as a whole, is a literary unity,[43] suggests that it is the only fully autobiographical Gospel. The facts elicited during this study appear to lead to the conclusion, alike from the literary, historical, and biographical points of view, that it comes from one

[41] *HFG*, 123.   [42] *HJ*, XLII.187.   [43] *FGH*, 35.

whose relationship with Jesus was so intimate, and his understanding of Him so clear, that he must have been one of the most favoured three among the disciples; one, moreover, of great spiritual susceptibility, enhanced by his coming under the influence of Jesus at exactly the most impressionable age;[44] who also accompanied Him on some or all of His visits to Jerusalem,[45] possibly from his first acquaintance with Him (1^{37}, $2^{1, 12}$, etc.), perhaps as His personal attendant and, it may be, confidant; and who survived until near the close of the first century A.D., with the consequent opportunity to think things through to their depths,[46] so that he was able more clearly than any other to apprehend the meaning of the facts he had observed in connexion with Jesus. James Drummond,[47] in a review of B. W. Bacon's *Fourth Gospel*, writes: '. . . one who had been the intimate friend of a great teacher . . . would be more likely to present a portrait stamped with his own individuality than a later biographer who had to rely on material which was well known and regarded as authentic.' But although John composed his Gospel in his old age as a sacred legacy he did not himself publish it to the Church, but left it in such a form that it had to be edited by others—probably the leaders of the Church at Ephesus.[48]

Any 'form-criticism' of John must be of a character different from that relating to the other Gospels.[49] In them there is scope for the alteration of a saying or incident in its passage from one mind or mouth to another. But if our conclusion is sound that here we have an understanding eye-witness, the only change of 'form' will be that which went on in his own mind. Sir F. Kenyon[50] says: 'The language may no doubt have been coloured

---

[44] *FGH*, 42–3, 83.   [45] ibid., 40–1.   [46] cf. *HFG*, 131; also *FGH*, 80.
[47] *HJ*, IX.199.   [48] *FGH*, 67.   [49] cf. *DJL*, 12.
[50] *The Reading of the Bible*, 61.

by passing through the mind of St John over a long period of years. . . .' In this sense, of course, he has given us an 'interpretation' of Jesus.[51] Of this there can be no doubt. The stories had been told again and again, and not only their outward expression, but also the shades of meaning and emphasis gradually altered as the whole set of ideas arranged themselves into a coherent system in the author's mind.[52]   J. A. Robinson[53] says: 'The old disciple . . . knows the Christ far better now than he knew him in Galilee or Jerusalem half a century before.'

That this Gospel differs so much from the other three is due to the author's special purpose. The Synoptists record for the most part the outward story of the ministry of Jesus, and their works contain incidents and teaching, including many aphoristic sayings, such as would most easily be retained in the popular mind; but John's aim is far from any mere record of outward things: he deliberately chooses the deep things which the popular mind did not retain or even understand, and wrote what is distinctly not a 'Life of Christ', but a monograph containing a selection of incidents chosen to illustrate a definite theme, as 20[31] shows quite clearly.[54]   F. Palmer[55] says: 'His work . . . is not a biography of Jesus, not a history of the events of his time; but the author aimed to demonstrate that Jesus was the Messiah and the Son of God, and this not so much for intellectual conviction as for spiritual edification.' While the other Gospels treat the facts simply as facts, this enables us to see the facts through the eyes of one who had gradually come to perceive their inner meaning, and who wrote, as he himself says, 'that you may believe that Jesus is the Christ, the Son of God, and that, believing, you may have life in his name'.

[51] cf. *SFG*, 17–18.   [52] cf. *FGH*, 75.   [53] *The Study of the Gospels*, 148.
[54] *FGH*, 3–4.   [55] *HJ*, V.609.